How to Price a Profitable Company

Second Edition

D1608643

How to Price a Profitable Company

Second Edition

Paul Baron

amacom
American Management Association
New York · Atlanta · Boston · Chicago · Kansas City · San Francisco · Washington, D. C.
Brussels · Mexico City · Tokyo · Toronto

This book is available at a special
discount when ordered in bulk quantities.
For information, contact Special Sales Department,
AMACOM, a division of American Management Association,
1601 Broadway, New York, NY 10019.

This publication is designed to provide accurate and authoritative
information in regard to the subject matter covered. It is sold with the
understanding that the publisher is not engaged in rendering legal,
accounting, or other professional service. If legal advice or other expert
assistance is required, the services of a competent professional person
should be sought.

Library of Congress Cataloging-in-Publication Data

Baron, Paul B.
     How to price a profitable company / Paul Baron.—2nd ed.
       p. cm.
     Includes bibliographical references and index.
     ISBN 0-8144-7910-3
     1. Close corporations—Valuation.   I. Title.
HG4028.V3B22   1996
658.15—dc20   96-15347
                                                   CIP

Printing number

10 9 8 7 6 5 4 3 2 1

Contents

Contents

List of Exhibits

Abbreviations
and
Acronyms

B.I.G. (statement)	belief in God (statement)
C.I.A.	cash in advance
EBIT	earnings before interest and taxes
EBDIT	earnings before depreciation, interest, and taxes
ESOP	employee stock ownership plan
f/c	free and clear
G.A.A.P.	generally accepted accounting principles
G.S. and A.	general, selling, and administrative expenses
IPO	initial public offering
IRR	internal rate of return
LBO	leveraged buyout
MBO	management buyout
P/E	price-earnings ratio
P&L	profit and loss
R&D	research and development
ROE	return on equity
ROI	return on investment
SBIC	Small Business Investment Company
SIC	standard industrial classification
T&C	travel and entertainment

Preface

Y OU have picked up this book because you want to sell your company, or because you want to buy a company, or because you are an intermediary who is helping a client buy or sell a company. However, you may be wondering whether the author of this book is qualified to give you the information you need.

I am a deal maker and intermediary who helps clients who want to buy or sell profitable, privately held manufacturing, distributing, or retail companies, generally in the size range of sales from $1.5–30 million. For such deal-making, I am engaged as an intermediary, a merger consultant, a broker, or finder. In addition, I also give "second opinions" on what I believe are reasonable selling prices for companies, on the basis of my knowledge and experience in the marketplace.

I was a retailer for 34 years and sold the business at age 55. My retirement lasted about one year, until by chance I sold a company for a friend and discovered the excitement known to businesspeople who want to buy or sell a company. I've been at it now for 19 years. For 20 years, I have been a director of a bank with footings of $500 million, serving on the executive committee, the trust committee, and as chairman of the audit committee. I am a member of the Association for Corporate Growth (New York Chapter).

While working toward my Executive M.B.A. (which I received at age 61), I became intrigued with the issue of reasonable price. How do sellers of companies arrive at their selling price? I researched this issue for one and a half years and finally put most of what I learned into a manual entitled *When You Buy or Sell a Company: How to Price and How to Negotiate.** To date, the sales of this manual have exceeded $1 million. I have also sold millions of dollars' worth of companies, almost always from a private seller to a private buyer.

I would like to acknowledge and thank the following for their help in writing this book: owners of all size businesses, deal-making lawyers, deal-making accountants, bankers, investment bankers, academics, appraisers, valuators, merger-and-acquisition executives, analysts, strategic planners, heads of development, a network of merger intermediaries, trade association executives, trust officers, and retired IRS Estate and Gift Tax Division agents.

*Stony Creek, Conn.: Center for Business Information.

How to Price a Profitable Company

Second Edition

Introduction
to the
Introduction

A MAJOR purpose of this book is to give you insight about reaching a reasonable and realistic market price for a profitable company to be sold or bought.

Whenever the masculine gender (he or him) is used, it is for ease of grammatical presentation only, and such reference shall be understood to include the feminine gender (she or her).

Introduction

A FRIEND recently amazed me by saying that he had just sold his business for about twice what he thought it was worth. He thought if he ever sold the company he could expect to receive about $4.5–5 million. Instead, he sold it for $9 million! My friend had not been in the market to sell; the buyer had come to him, especially wanting the seller's marketing organization for his existing and allied businesses. Crazy things once in a while, but not too often.

Someone comes to you and asks if you would be interested in selling your business. If you have not been thinking or acting like a seller, you are in a position to say in truth, "I haven't been thinking about selling. But tell me what's it worth to you, and I'll consider it." But if you have already decided to sell and you then offer your company for sale, you will be expected to give your offering price.

Getting to the offering price is what this book is about. Why is it needed? *Because most sellers do not know how to set a reasonable, realistic price* for the company they want to sell. They are in uncharted waters. The owners have shown their intelligence by developing and operating a profitable company. Now how do they go about intelligently selling a price for the company they want to sell?

In addition to selling or buying a company, there are many other reasons why someone might need a price for a company. The price is determined by the purpose. You could end up with about ten different prices, all with their own rationale, depending on the purpose in setting a price.

Here is a partial list of why prices are sometimes needed:

- To determine estate or gift taxes
- For valuation of a fractional part of a business
- In case of a divorce
- To set the value of intangible assets, such as patents, trademarks, mailing lists, subscribers
- For condemnation
- To conduct feasibility studies
- In case of litigation
- To put up collateral
- To determine insurance values
- To arrive at buy-and-sell agreements

This book teaches you how to set a reasonable price for a profitable, privately held manufacturing, distribution, or retail company with sales from about $1.5–30 million, or with (normalized) earnings from about $250,000 to $3.5 million, to be sold as a going concern. The methods we arrive at are those used by sophisticated, experienced, fair buyers and their support staff, who are active in the market.

In my experience, most companies that are offered for sale do not sell. The reason they do not sell is because the price is too high to be reasonable or realistic. I think some of the practices that most often lead to unrealistic prices are:

- Using the Treasury or IRS methods, which are required in valuations in cases of death (estate) and gifts.
- Aggressiveness on the part of sellers or brokers where the annual growth of sales and earnings is under 15%. Many times exponential earnings are projected and a high, high price is promised. Most of the professional buyers I know do not pay, or do not pay up front, for *potential.*
- Advice from a professional who is not a deal maker, or not very experienced in the marketplace. Such professionals know how to value a company for purposes of estate or gift tax but not as a going concern.
- Sellers who cannot forget their start-up costs and research expenses and are determined to recoup what has been spent.
- Sellers who decide what they need for living expenses and determine the price by those needs.
- An attempt to apply the price/earnings (P/E) ratios of the public market to the sale of private companies.

The last practice is particularly significant. There is no question that the pricing of privately held companies is influenced by pricing of public companies. But which private companies can compare themselves with the crème de la crème of the public companies that command high P/Es in the marketplace? There are about 50,000 publicly held companies in the United States, of which in recent years only 200 had annual growth of over 25%.

There are no comparables in the sale of private companies.

There is no central agency, no requirement to file a report, no disclosure requirements about what company sold for how much. Most of the time the intermediary must assure the seller that he or she will keep all the elements of the sale confidential and not reveal to anyone how the deal was cut up. Only the insiders know the terms applying to any consultancy agreements, employment contracts, interest rates, perks, earnouts, or covenants not to compete. And the biggest problem in pricing private companies, of course, is trying to dig out information about the earnings.

This book takes you on a journey, to arrive at a reasonable price for a company you want to sell or buy. The early chapters discuss buyers and sellers, valuation and pricing, traditional but unacceptable methods of pricing companies, and general capital budgeting techniques and terms. Our journey then takes us to Chapters 5 and 6—the "meat and potatoes" of the book—on reaching the reasonable price. Chapter 7 covers negotiating skills, and Chapter 8 presents deal killers and reasons why companies don't sell.

The thrust and emphasis of this book is on companies with specific characteristics:

1. They are privately held, closely held, or family held.
2. They have revenues from about $1.5–30 million. However, the techniques for EBIT (earnings before interest and taxes) pricing discussed in Chapters 5 and 6 apply not only to companies in that range but to all mid-sized companies, that is, companies with sales from $1–75 million.
3. They are profitable. There is nothing in this book about turnarounds, companies that are losing money, or companies that have a loss carryforward.

1

About Buyers
and
Sellers

The seller thinks he sold too cheaply, and the buyer thinks he paid too much.

The most important benefit provided by a broker is pointing the prospect in the right direction, at the right time.

—*Fred Board*

The worst time to sell a company is when you have to.

I T has been said that the ideal company for sale has these four characteristics:

1. It has lots of excess cash flow.
2. The owner can deliver all the ownership.
3. The owner wants to sell.
4. The asset value exceeds the purchase price.

But since no one can find such a company, we compromise: We deal with reality.

The reality is that there is a very dynamic market for the sale of all kinds of companies. It is estimated that 20% of all businesses change hands each year. Good, profitable companies are in particularly high demand, and some of the reasons for all that activity can be seen in the statistics in Exhibit 1-1.

The principal players in the buying and selling of companies are obviously the buyer and the seller, and in this chapter we discuss both groups. We look at who these diverse players are, and at what motivates them. For the purposes of this book, let us assume that the buyers and sellers are negotiating to buy or sell a profitable company, not a company that is in trouble, not one in chapter 11 bankruptcy, and not a turnaround.

First, let us look at buyers.

Buyers

There are different sorts of buyers, and they operate differently. Their motivations and methods generally depend on whether they are strategic buyers or financial buyers. We also consider the special conditions involved in dealing with foreign buyers, and we must discuss the specialists: the professional buyers.

Strategic Buyers

Strategic buyers want to add on, diversify, or expand into new businesses as part of a long-term strategic plan. They are interested in your company* because:

*For the sake of simplicity, in this book I favor implying that you the reader are a seller, although (as the Preface and Introduction note) you might in fact have a buyer's interest.

Exhibit 1-1. Statistics backing the reasons profitable companies are in high demand.

- In 1982, there were 475,000 millionaires in the United States. A recent study indicates that there are now about two million millionaires. Among the richest are self-employed persons and owners of businesses.

- It is estimated that there are one million businesses with sales of $1–5 million, and there are 30,000 businesses with sales of $5–60 million.

- Of the Fortune 500 companies, 150, or almost one-third, are privately held, closely held, or family held.

- Of the 14 million tax returns for businesses, 2.9 million are for corporations, of which only 50,000 are publicly held. Ninety-nine percent of the 14 million returns are for small companies, with sales of less than $500,000.

- The IRS defines a large corporation as one with $10 million in assets.

- The mortality rate of new businesses is high: two out of three start-ups close in the first year, and four out of five close within five years.

- Finally, a recent study of Harvard Business School M.B.A.s showed that 18 years after graduation, 40% of the class had become entrepreneurs, with an average annual compensation of $450,000. That's about twice the average income of those who were doing similar work in industry as employees, not as entrepreneurs.

- They are in the same kind of business but in a different part of the country, and they want to expand into your geographic area, or
- Your company is a synergistic fit that rounds out their product lines, or
- They are interested in your sales organization, your skills as direct marketers, or your customers, or
- They are interested in your technology.

In other words, your company is a good fit, and they understand your business.

Some executives have as strategic goals to double the size of their company in five years and to increase their earnings. To achieve these goals, their company must grow aggressively, either internally or, more likely, externally by way of mergers or acquisitions. As a result, there is a big demand for good companies. For example, one CEO of a major corporation speaks of his two major responsibilities as:

1. Planning for the succession of top officers (i.e., who is going to fill so-and-so's shoes) and cultivating a group of young managers
2. Planning how to allocate the company's funds and resources: where it should invest its money, and what companies it should acquire

Other executives are concerned about future changes in the market or in their customer base. At a recent meeting of mergers-and-acquisitions people, someone told me that she worked in the business planning section. Her major responsibility was to try to determine who their customers would be in the years 2000 and 2005, and what they would want to buy.

Strategic buyers usually have a sense of urgency, because they need what the seller has—a product line, a sales organization, a customer base—and they need it as soon as possible.

Financial Buyers

The *financial buyer* is one who looks to make an acquisition because it makes sense in financial terms. Financial buyers are interested in your company because it is a good investment for their company. It can be a freestanding investment, not related to any other investment. For example:

- Your company will add steady, consistent earnings, or
- Your company's earnings are growing at a higher rate than the buying company's earnings, or
- Your company can be grown and sold at a profit.

In the beginning, financial buyers may or may not understand the new business. They understand *finance*. There are those whose personal wealth provides closing power, as well as those whose purchasing power is determined by how much they can raise at the bank. Some have the capacity to do a deal for cash, and some might even bring their banker along in the early conversations. Some have very little money or no money; their credo is "OK. Your price, our terms."

Most financial buyers do not want to operate the company, and they generally will not buy the company unless satisfactory management is in place. Some buyers just want to be the chairman of the board and show up on occasion. They may want to determine the direction the company is to move in, help develop the strategic plan, set the financial controls, or help with the marketing. Maybe they do the same thing for a dozen companies they own.

However, other financial buyers actually do want to operate the company and are looking forward to having operating responsibility and being hands-on owners. Today there are a lot of buyers out there who have been professional managers and now want to run their own company. They might have been laid off or gotten the golden handshake, and they need or want to go back to work. They feel that by owning a company they'll be in charge of their own future. It is estimated that 30% of the current prospects for franchises are recently terminated corporate executives.

On the other hand, you might find a very hot prospect, just raring to buy a company—maybe any company—and he or she has the money to do so. This prospective buyer might have been on the verge of closing on one or more companies, but things happened at the last moment and he lost the deal. The seller might have backed out, or another buyer might have walked in and closed the deal. This prospect came in second best, and he is frustrated. Things have not gone his way, his ego is bruised, and he is determined not to let the next situation get away from him. He now realizes how difficult it is to find a really good company. So Mr. or Ms. Buyer is hot and wants to close a deal.

Foreign Buyers

There are many prospective *foreign buyers* for U.S. companies. They may be strategic or financial buyers, or a combination of both. Foreign buyers have two important advantages over American buyers:

1. They usually enjoy a favorable foreign exchange rate, so it's easier for them to bid higher prices.
2. In many countries, their tax code permits them to deduct the full goodwill (defined in brief as the difference between the selling price and tangible assets) in the year of the purchase. Until 1993, U.S. companies got no deduction for goodwill and many other intangibles. Now U.S. companies can amortize goodwill over a 15-year period, as a deductible expense.

Professional Buyers

Buyers are either *professional buyers* or individual investors. Professional buyers might include the merger-and-acquisition executives of companies, individuals or groups who might own three or five or ten different companies, or holding companies.

Professional buyers know what the marketplace is like and what the competition is like. There is a certain method to the way they look at a company. Professional buyers know exactly what they are looking for, and they can provide the specifications and criteria for the kind of company that they want to buy.

On the other hand, individual investors for the most part have never bought (or sold) a company before. Inexperienced buyers, people who have never bought or sold a company, discover that there is a lot of education involved to learn what they never knew before.

People like me—business brokers, finders, merger consultants, and intermediaries—constantly receive mail and calls from people who want to buy companies. We do not have a bag full of companies for sale. We might only have a few good ones that we are working on. So we are not going to reveal anything about those candidate companies unless we are sure that the prospective buyers have the capacity to close a deal, are serious buyers, will not violate any confidentiality, and understand the business.

Acquisition Criteria

If brokers and intermediaries do not know enough about a prospective buyer, they generally ask for the buyer's acquisition criteria. They will probably ask to have them in writing. Typical criteria include the following elements:

1. *Sales.* What range of sales or minimum sales level is the buyer interested in? It could be expressed as:
   - $1–5 million, or
   - $5–10 million, or
   - Minimum $10 million
2. *Earnings or cash flow from the prospective acquisition.* It could be expressed as:
   - Minimum $500,000, or
   - Minimum $1 million, or
   - Minimum $2 million, or
   - 10% on sales
3. *Management.* What does the buyer want to do with the existing management? This criterion could be variously expressed as:
   - Have management stay and run the company, or
   - Have the owner leave, or
   - Have the owner stay for training, or
   - Have motivated management, not caretaker management
4. *Selling price.* The buyer may express this criterion generally or specifically:
   - In a range that is reasonable and realistic, or

- 50% of the purchase price should be borrowable against the balance sheet
5. *Geography.* The buyer would like a company that is located, for example:
   - Anywhere in the United States, or
   - In the Southwest, or
   - No farther than 150 miles from Philadelphia, or
   - In Ohio
6. *Form of payment.* The criterion could be to:
   - Pay cash, or
   - Use some seller financing
7. *The kind of business* the buyer does or does not want:
   - A company with a proprietary product or niche, or
   - A company with a specific SIC* classification, or
   - A company with strength in, for example, the mail-order business
8. *Earnings criteria.* These can be expressed in numerous forms:
   - Look for net after-tax profits of 12% (equals 20% pretax)
   - Should be a potential public issue in three to five years
   - Must have minimum ROI of 15%
   - Need consistent pretax earnings of 14% on sales, with growth

Sellers

Sellers are not as easily categorized as buyers. They have a wide variety of reasons for wanting to sell their companies.

In this section, we review different reasons why sellers want to sell. We also discuss the best time to sell a company.

Why Sellers Want to Sell Their Companies

Here are 25 reasons, any one of which a seller might give for putting a company up for sale. Each reason given here is a com-

---

*Standard Industrial Classification. The government divides all businesses into 10 major classifications and hundreds of subclassifications. Every C-corporation IRS form contains the SIC number for the company filing the tax returns.

posite of real-life answers and situations that I have encountered.

1. "I'm tired. I've been at it 35 years."
2. "I promised my wife I'd quit when I was 65."
3. "I'm sick."
4. "None of my family is interested in our business." *or* "My children are not suited to run the company."
5. "I want to get my estate in order." Most older businesspeople can tell you they know one or two business families in which a principal died unexpectedly, and the family had to sell the company for a disappointing price.
6. "The company needs lots of money to expand (or grow or upgrade), and at my age I don't want to go back into debt."
7. "There are management problems (or divorce problems, family problems, minority stockholder problems, employee problems). "I knew of one family business with 60 stockholders ranging in age from five months to 90 years. The diverse goals and interests became impossible to reconcile, so they sold the company.
8. "I have other opportunities."
9. "I'd like to merge. My company is growing too fast for me, and for our resources. I can't (or don't want to) handle these growth problems at this stage of my life."
10. "Two key people are leaving." *or* "My manager is retiring in two years." *or* "A key person died."
11. "Someone came along with an offer I can't refuse."
12. "I have an opportunity to go into another business. It's bigger." *or* "It's more of a challenge." *or* "My father-in-law wants me to take over his company." (All three may all be true.)
13. "The neighborhood is becoming too dangerous; there have been acts of violence, crime, vandalism, fire. The working atmosphere is uncomfortable, and I don't want to deal with those problems anymore."
14. "I am losing my drive, my sense of competitiveness. I may also be beginning to lose my confidence."
15. "I have enough money and feel financially independent."

16. "I'd like to sell out to my executives, but they don't have enough money, and they haven't been able to get someone to help with a management buyout (MBO). I don't want an installment sale—I want my money at the closing."
17. "The company is growing too fast, and it needs a new kind of manager to take the company to the next plateau."
18. "There is trouble brewing with environmental problems, labor problems, and legislative problems. I don't want to deal with them."
19. "I'll sell if I can get enough IFCOME (not income). That is, I'll sell if I can get enough income from the proceeds of the sale to maintain my style of spending, after taxes and inflation, and including my perks. If I can't sell, I'll have to continue to work."
20. "I want to diversify. I don't want everything in one basket."
21. "I have an opportunity to become part of something bigger."
22. "I want to be able to play golf all year long." *or* "I want to move to a different part of the country."
23. "I want a new kind of independence. I want to paint (or play music, or travel, or take time off when I want to)."
24. "I think it's great to have a tax-free exchange of stock with a solid public company."
25. *Best of all:* "I'm ready to sell."

What Is the Ideal Time to Sell Your Company? (In a Perfect World)

The best time to sell your company is when your company is "hot," when your earnings and sales are in a continuing period of super growth. Keep in mind that sustained super growth cannot last forever. In terms of the life cycle of a business, the period when the growth curve is the steepest is usually in the company's adolescent and mature periods. Buyers are looking for attractive, profitable companies, and big premiums are paid for companies with above-average growth.

Sometimes the world is less than perfect. You may want (or need) to sell at a point other than the adolescent and mature periods. In order to get a good price, you have to show a history of earnings and a future promise of good earnings. You could get a big price from an employee or a close relative who has worked for you and knows the real world inside the business. But a buyer who is a stranger will not pay for earnings she can't see, and the place she will look for information is in the IRS returns, or the financial and cash-flow statements.

In this unfair world, there may be times when a business must be sold on an emergency basis; the business has to be sold in a hurry and without being suitably prepared for presentation. In cases where there is a death or serious illness, or severe competition, or where the owner is plain tired, the business is likely to be sold at a low price, unless it is unusually profitable or attractive.

2
About Value and Pricing

It's not how much you pay, but how you pay it.

One should not get too carried away with more theoretical approaches to valuation, but be very conscious of what is happening in the real world and know the prices at which businesses are being bought and sold in the marketplace.

—*J. Murray Armitage*

Sometimes one man's treasure is another man's trash, and sometimes one man's trash is another man's treasure. But sometimes one man's treasure is another man's treasure.

RECENTLY, the owner of a small medical-products distributorship called to discuss the pricing of his company, which he said he might want to sell. The bare bones figures were:

Sales: $3 million, level and consistent for three years
Pretax income and benefits: $250,000

Tangible net worth: $750,000
Management: no real depth

The owner mentioned that he had just returned from a seminar on buying and selling companies, where he was told that he should be able to get about $3 million for his company. When I asked why anyone would be willing to pay him $3 million for a business earning $250,000 pretax, he said the seminar leader had explained that a new owner could "explode" his existing sales (since the present owner had been holding back the expansion of the company), and that he, the present owner, should be reimbursed for organizing the business, developing the computer programs, and many other intangibles. When I told him I thought that a reasonable price for his company would be about $1 million, he was not happy about my interpretation. But he accepted it—I think.

> *Most businesses offered for sale do not sell because they are overpriced, or because they do not make enough money to justify the selling price and the debt service.*

On Valuation

There are many ways to assess the value of a business, depending on *who* is doing the appraisal and *why* it is being done.

What is something worth? What is its value?

The value depends on the purpose. For example:

- What is the *perceived value* of your business?
- What is the *asset value* of your business?
- What is the *absolute value* of your business?
- What is the *real value* of your business?
- What is the *economic value* of your business?

Believe it or not, you will find no definitions of perceived value, asset value, absolute value, true value, real value, or economic value in Kohler's *Dictionary for Accountants*.* Webster, however, defines *worth* as "material value, especially as expressed in terms of money or some other medium of exchange."

Definitions

There are definitions that are used variously by appraisers, insurance people, and estate planners. Let's look at some of these definitions.

appraised value (or depreciated reproduction costs) Cost or value established by appraisal, at a price realized between a willing buyer and a willing seller in an open market. This value is an opinion, by a recognized and experienced person, of the market value of something to be sold, at a particular time and under different conditions.

Generally, for appraisals of equipment and machinery the appraiser gives an opinion of the value of the property *in place, operating, and debugged*. The value is at cost of reproduction less observed depreciation.

Obviously, it is important that the appraiser have no financial interest in the appraised property.

(net) book value Original costs, less depreciation, according to the corporate method of taking depreciation. Book value usually has little relationship to fair market value. Generally, when analyzing the fair market value a good place to start is with the book value, to which all kinds of adjustments are then made. Probably very few businesses are ever sold at book value, but it is a reference point.

conditional value The value that will ensue if a particular event occurs. For example, suppose a company has been bidding on a very large contract that could result in exceptional earnings. The owner could say to a prospective buyer, "I'll sell the company for X dollars, but if we get that contract you'll have to pay an additional amount."

*Eric L. Kohler, *A Dictionary for Accountants*, Fifth Edition. (Englewood Cliffs, NJ: Prentice-Hall, 1975).

expected value   A weighted average of all values conditional upon an act or event. Each conditional value is weighted by its probability.

fair market value (as defined by the IRS)   That price at which a willing buyer buys and a willing seller sells a certain item of property, neither being under any compulsion to buy or to sell and both having a reasonable knowledge of all relevant facts.

going-concern value   Owner's equity in a business enterprise. The very technical definition taken from Kohler's *Dictionary for Accountants:* Going-concern value differs from market value or worth of a business entity, as in a prospective disposal or business combination, such worth often being the result of a complex of imponderable, subjectively determined values emerging from consideration of future earning power, product demand, competitive strength, present and prospective governmental regulatory restraints, bargaining concessions, and so on.*

insurance terms relating to values   Generally, when you obtain a real estate appraisal for insurance purposes, the appraisal does not include land, foundations, or special underground utilities. Therefore, these values need to be added back into the appraisal to get a total value of the real property. You must make sure that you know what is "excluded." Your insurance company can give you the exclusions in writing.

intangible asset   The value of a going concern less the net tangible assets. Intangible assets arise from patents, trademarks, secret processes, subscription lists, copyrights, monopoly, or goodwill. Intangible assets that have measurable life (for example, the remaining life of a patent) are depreciable.

Insurance appraisals are used in establishing the value of a company or the allocation of assets after a sale.

Here are several important definitions of terms commonly used by insurance appraisers:

actual cash value   This term is used in insurance policies but is almost never defined in the policy. In many states, courts

*Kohler, p. 236. Reprinted with permission.

have different interpretations. It is best to check whether a policy carries an endorsement for *reproduction* cost or for *replacement* cost. Check with your agent. How would your insurance company settle?

cost of reproduction new   The amount to replace new in exactly like kind.

liquidation value   The amount an item would bring under a forced sale within a specific time frame. Generally, this value is the price you could expect if the business were closed down. In one situation, a company wanted to give a $6 million subsidiary company free to anyone who would take over the plant and continue to run it. It seems that their union contract required severance pay and full funding of the pension plan in the event the plant was to be closed, and that would have exceeded $9 million. (Incidentally, there were no takers.)

market value   The recent invoice or quoted price.

original cost   The invoice price or purchase price. It may or may not include tax, freight, or labor.

replacement costs   The cost to replace the property with a new, modern version of equivalent capacity or utility. It considers modern materials, modern design concepts, and modern technology. It can be more than reproduction cost, or it can be less. It would likely be the same as reproduction cost.

sound insurable value   Sound value less the exclusions.

sound value   Cost of reproduction new less an allowance for depreciation.

subjective value   The value to a person based on an emotional reason, regardless of its worth to another.

tax basis   Used for federal tax purposes, this is capitalized cost less depreciation as permitted by IRS code. It may or may not be the same as book value.

The kind of valuation clearly depends on its purpose. For example, if you want to finance some of your machinery equipment, the bank may be very interested in the liquidation value. For insurance purposes, the insurance company wants to know about actual cash values, replacement values, production values, or sound values. For your corporate records and taxes, you need to know about book value, tax basis, and depreciated re-production costs.

In general, when it comes to the buying or selling of a business, you will keep hearing about fair market value. Nine out of 10 times, however, businesses are not sold at fair market value. When a member of the American Society of Appraisers gives you an appraisal, he or she will tell you that this is *opinion*, a theoretical value.

Appraisal Methods

A lawyer friend of mine had her first job with a Wall Street law firm. One of her first assignments was to work with a team to value a railroad. She went to see one of the partners to inquire how a railroad is valued. His first question to her was, "For what purpose do you need the valuation? The value depends on the purpose."

Most professional appraisers use one or more of four methods:

1. Methods based on *asset values,* where the assets are adjusted from book value to current fair market value.
2. Those based on *earnings.* Appraisers might give examples and work-ups involving discounted future earnings, capitalized earnings, and price/earnings ratios.
3. Those based on public *stock market comparisons,* using P/E ratios or dividend ratios, or information from recent mergers.
4. Those based on discounted cash flow (DCF) or *present-value* methods, using cash flows, terminal values, and discount rates.

There are also miscellaneous rule-of-thumb or formula methods, as we discuss in Chapter 3. Note, however, that most professional buyers do not rely on a formal appraisal when deciding on their price. It is always earnings and the consistency of earnings that are the key determinants.

Pricing

The phrase that describes the price a business is sold for is not even listed in Kohler's dictionary. It is the negotiated purchase price.

The Negotiated Purchase Price

The negotiated purchase price is the amount and the terms and conditions at which the transfer takes place. The amount finally agreed to by the seller and the buyer, it covers such questions as:

> How much is to be paid now
> How much is to be paid later
> How the amount is to be paid
> Whether interest is actual or imputed
> Who pays what expenses
> Under what conditions

Do not confuse fair market value with the negotiated purchase price. Sometimes they may be the same, but hardly ever. Fair market value is theory; it is opinion. Do the buyer and seller ever have full and perfect knowledge? Will the buyer see the company in exactly the same way as the seller? The negotiated purchase price is the "horse-trade" price.

Seven Different Kinds of Prices

In the nomenclature of buying and selling companies, the negotiated purchase price is just one of seven types of prices generally talked about. They are:

1. *Seller's asking price.* The seller will be ecstatic.
2. *Seller's bull's-eye or target price.* A happy seller.
3. *Seller's sacrifice price.* This price will not make the seller happy, but it is probably above the liquidation value, and it may give him some other kind of benefit. It may

be a way to lock up a good lease, so if he is pressed and can see the benefit, he may accept.

4. *The negotiated price.* The horse-trade price.
5. *The floor price.* The price below which the seller will not sell, because it does not fulfill his objectives.
6. *The buyer's "walk-away price"* (or *"tip-over price"*). This is the absolute ceiling the buyer will pay. Anything higher would be unacceptable and not permit him to fulfill his financial objectives. He would in fact walk away above this price, because the company is not worth any more to him unless he can be convinced otherwise. The seller usually does not know what the buyer's walk-away price is until he gets there. In general, buyers do not start at the walk-away price because they want to buy the company for less.

   Sometimes buyers pay more than such a price, usually when there is an overriding psychological or emotional reason. The buyer may feel he must be boss of a certain company or type of company, or that he is a man or woman of destiny, or that he or she has to prove a point, or that he or she can succeed where others have failed.
7. *The buyer's take-it-or-leave-it price.* The buyer hopes that it is an offer that cannot be refused.

Successful buyers and negotiators all have their own ways of looking at prices. For example:

> One veteran of many successful real estate deals says it very well:

> The buyer makes the offer, the seller accepts, and that's the market price.

> An entrepreneur who has made four sizable acquisitions says:

> I like to give my price. I do my homework and analysis. I figure what it's worth to me and that's it. I don't have time to haggle, and I don't like to haggle. If I buy it, I buy it. If I don't, I don't.

A prominent negotiator for a multinational company has yet another point of view:

> If someone wants to pay more than you do, that doesn't mean you were wrong.

On the other hand, a well-known negotiator for a multinational company almost never gives a first price, preferring instead to bargain for every deal.

As Ray Bolger used to say, "It depends on how you look at things."

Competitive Information

Prices are a product of current deals, that is, what comparable companies are being sold for. Unfortunately, there is no place like the New York Stock Exchange, or *The Wall Street Journal*, where you can get public information on deals involving privately held companies. As a matter of fact, the terms under which most private companies are sold are confidential; hardly anyone knows the details, and that is the way the seller wants it: *confidential*. There is no requirement for disclosure. It is difficult to find people who know what is going on in the marketplace of privately held companies. But the professionals who do know that market would probably be:

1. Deal-making lawyers who devote a substantial part of their practice to clients who are buying or selling businesses.
2. Deal-making accountants. Same remarks as in item 1.
3. Deal-making bankers. Same remarks as in item 1.
4. Principals in holding companies that buy and sell companies for their own account.
5. Knowledgeable brokers, intermediaries, and investment bankers who know the marketplace.
6. SBIC (Small Business Investment Company) lenders who finance private company purchases, and knowledgeable cash-flow and asset-based lenders.
7. Deal makers and intermediaries. These are people who are in the marketplace. They understand and know what prices are being paid by knowledgeable buyers.

The buyers I know do not set a price based on an appraisal, based on acceptable legal and accounting methods. They are not concerned with methods or pricing as used in the courts. They are not rule-of-thumb buyers; they are not discounted cash-flow buyers. They are also not interested in setting a price that is related to the cost of setting up the company.

Setting a Price

Prices are influenced by many factors:

Good luck and timing
Earnings (they need to be predictable and sustainable)
Terms: money now, later, or contingency
Enthusiasm by seller
Strategic value
Presentation
Negotiating skills
Need to sell: health, psychological, or emotional factors
Risk of not getting paid
Taxes
Ability to survive debt
Cost of money
Growth rate
Ability of buyer to close
How badly the buyer wants to buy
How badly the seller wants to sell
Supply and demand
The economy
Financials
Life cycle of the business

The price is generally not a single figure, but rather a price range with a top and a bottom. The intermediary's job is to find a buyer, if possible, who is willing to pay the higher price because he understands the rationale for a higher price and thinks that way. There is a rationale for why the selling company fits into the top or bottom of the range. What special qualities does the selling company have or not have? Will the seller start at the top of the range, and will the buyer start at the bottom? Will they strike a deal in the middle?

These are all factors in the negotiation. A profitable company's price will be based on a combination of the earnings and the underlying assets.

In most situations, it is the seller who sets the initial price—if he wants to sell, that is his responsibility. However, when a buyer's seeking out of an owner is unsolicited, it makes sense that the buyer make the first offer.

Different buyers have different perceptions about pricing. But professional buyers always think about pricing based on earnings on a *pretax* basis (not after-tax). Remember this:

THIS IS VERY IMPORTANT ©

> *Buyers must have a true picture of the earnings. Without those numbers, the parties are spinning their wheels. Without those numbers, there is no basis, no rationale for arriving at a selling price.*

Structuring the Deal

The seller must decide what he wants to sell before a price is set. This is what we call "how much for how much?" A company is not like real estate, where the offering is for a piece of land with improvements (a building) on it. A company can be sold many different ways. For example, it can be sold for a stock transaction, for all the assets and liabilities, for all of the assets, or for some of the assets (such as the operating assets, with or without the working capital). The buyer might assume all of the debt, or none of the debt.

The deal can be structured many different ways. It is impossible for an outsider to know what happens in the deal. You can cut up the deal, with so much going for the company, so much for the consultancy agreements, so much for employment agreements, and so much for interest-rate adjustments. The price can be for cash or for terms, broken up into noncompete agreements, advisory-services agreements, special rental agreements, earn-outs . . . whatever the human mind can dream up and whatever two parties agree on, so long as it is legal.

The tax situations of the buyer and seller also play a role in how the deal is structured. There are people who have been waiting eight years for the capital-gains rates to be reduced before they will sell their companies. Also, when the Big Six accounting firms send out lists of client companies that are for sale, those listings often show two offering prices: the first for a stock deal, and the second for an asset deal. The latter is probably at about a 20% higher price.

Public vs. Private Companies

The seller must understand that there is a marketplace out there, and prices have been established in the marketplace. However, very few people are intimately familiar with that marketplace. Thus there are companies that provide "fairness opinions." Such an opinion is required by public companies to protect the minority stockholders' interests. These provider companies usually offer a full range of valuation methodologies, including:

Comparative analysis
ROI investment analysis
Discounted cash flow
Liquidation
Break-up values
Replacement values

While these methods are suitable for public companies, they are not appropriate for the small and mid-sized, privately held companies. When we speak of earnings, we must remember that the points of view held by the owners of a private or closely held company on the one hand and a publicly held company on the other will differ.

A closely held company is supposed to be run for the benefit of the owner. Thus all the accounting practices and the structure of the company are designed to minimize taxes and to fulfill the owner's needs. Some owners are interested in getting the maximum financial rewards, and they work very hard at it. Some want community recognition. Some want more leisure time. Some don't want the company to grow. Some want to be men and women of "destiny and distinction." Some like things just as they are. An owner may feel he's rich enough, that he has enough income. An owner may feel that there is no point in risking his wealth for expansion or modernization, or in disturbing a lifestyle that he has worked so hard to achieve. Economists call this "satisfying."

The publicly held company cannot afford that kind of luxury or behavior. The publicly held company has a different mission: to increase the wealth of the company. Generally, the increase comes with an increase and growth in earnings, which generally are reflected in a higher market price for the stock and a higher P/E ratio.

It is very difficult to get information about what privately held companies have sold for. There are no disclosure requirements as there are for real estate, and the announcements of a sale or merger of privately held companies often carries the line: "The sales price and other terms of the purchase were not released." The comparables are available only to a small circle of professional buyers, deal-making lawyers, accountants, holding-company executives, specialty lending bankers, and merger-and-acquisition specialists.

Auctions

An auction is a unique illustration of this process of valuing and pricing a company. To see what it reveals about obtaining value information, let us examine how an investment banker would sell a division of a large company.

If the company has good earnings and good management, there will be plenty of buyers. Larger properties are generally put up at auction rather than sold on a negotiated basis; experts tell us that an auction brings a higher price. But this is not the kind of auction that you might envision—the prospective buyers are not invited into a room on the day of the auction to let the bidding start.

Here is how such an auction usually works.

1. The investment banking firm puts out a news release that such-and-such corporation has retained them to sell off a certain division (or a specific company).
2. This announcement puts the company into the market-

place (or "into play"). Prospective buyers begin notifying the investment bankers of their interest. Meanwhile, the staff of the investment banking firm starts developing their own list of prospects.

3. About a month after the announcement, the investment bankers send out a package of information to those they consider prospects. They might send out 50, 100, or 150 packages.

4. During the next month, those prospects who are seriously interested review the financial information, inspect the premises, perform their "due diligence," and talk to the managers. Those who remain seriously interested at this stage are considered finalists.

5. The finalists are ready to make their bid. They generally do not know who the other bidders are, or for that matter how many finalists there are. The finalists are told that the final bid must be in by a certain date, along with a supporting statement of how the deal is to be paid for or financed, and which financial institutions have made commitments to them. Those commitments must be made in advance, because the investment banker generally does not accept a bid from a prospect saying only that they will buy the company if they can get the money.

Leveraged Buyouts

The public market for leveraged buyouts (LBOs) tends to have a significant effect on the expectations of sellers of smaller companies. They may set unreasonable prices for their companies. As we shall see, the high prices paid in LBO transactions—where premiums average about 40% over market—are not appropriate in transactions involving smaller companies.

These days, a classic LBO occurs when a group of investors buys a company and takes it private. The investors take in the managers as minority-interest partners. The managers operate the company on a day-to-day basis, with the principal input of the major investors being in strategic planning and financial planning. It is estimated that there are nearly fifty buyout funds that can close on deals worth $1 billion or more.

The rewards are great to the successful. Kohlberg, Kravis, Roberts & Co. (KKR) is reported to have earned its pension fund investors compound annual returns to over 45% for nine years. Compare that with conventional investment returns of 10–12%. And it is not uncommon for an LBO to pay for 90% of the purchase price in debt financing.

What is all the excitement about? Simply that there is lots of money to be made—for everybody:

- For the *buyers:* They hope to realize at least 30–40% return. They expect to get five times their original investment in five years.
- For the *bankers:* They get about double the fees for buyout loans as for commercial loans.
- For the *investment bankers:* They expect to get advisory fees of 1% of the buyout price, and an extra 4% for lining up the financing. It is not uncommon for an investment banker to receive a bonus of five times salary.
- For the *managers:* They expect to get about 10–20% of equity, usually at the same price as the investors.
- For the *providers of the subordinated debt,* or mezzanine financing: Their portion is the riskiest part of the financing. They probably expect to receive three or four points over prime, and equity kickers that can run as high as 15% of the company. Generally, they do not require any repayment of principal for a long period, such as five years.

Financing an LBO

If you pay more than eight times earnings, you cannot service the debt without an increase in earnings (unless you have an extraordinary company). Connie Bruck writes* that in the Pantry Pride/Revlon deal, Drexel, Burnham, Lambert, Inc.'s boilerplate read: "Funds generated by existing operations will not be sufficient to enable the company to meet these obligations."

What happens, then, in many cases is:

- Some assets are sold off to raise cash and pay off part of the debt.

*Connie Bruck, *The Predator's Ball* (New York: Simon & Schuster, 1988).

- The expenses start getting controlled more stringently.
- Capital expenses are frozen.
- Overhead is cut.
- Incentives are put in place.

The real trick is in doing the financing. In general, LBO deals are extremely complex and therefore appropriate only for very large companies. Deals involving companies with sales between $1.5 million and $30 million most likely could *not* be done with the kind of financing normally used in LBOs. Consequently the seller of a smaller company should not expect to get the larger price that an LBO transaction commands.

To illustrate the complexity of an LBO, here are the financing components of a recent deal. All of these components were required in order to raise enough money for the purchase price, the transaction costs, and working capital.

Equity by the investors and management:	4.0%
Quasi equity:	4.0%
Guaranteed note:	26.0%
Subordinated notes:	10.0%
Preferred stock:	22.0%
Term loan:	8.0%
Revolving loan:	26.0%

Harold Geneen, the great master of deal-making, once explained how he could arrive at a premium price that could be used to set the price in an LBO. In his example, a company has earnings of $1 a share and a market price of $12 a share. The $1 per share is after-tax, equivalent to $1.67 pretax in the 40% tax bracket. Geneen stated that every $1 in after-tax earnings would pay the interest on a $21 loan. In other words, for every $1 earned on that one company he could borrow an additional $21, enough to make dozens of additional deals.

Nowadays, the average debt-to-equity ratio in the largest public industrial companies is about 2 to 1. In total, the proportion of corporate debt to equity is 88%, and the debt service is 40% of cash flow. Many LBOs have a debt-to-equity ratio of 5 to 1, some even 8 to 1.

As one sagacious investor said: "One-third of our deals come from Wall Street. The auction market is very difficult. You know you paid the highest possible price [in an auction]—higher than anyone else is willing to pay for the company."

Says another investor: "If we can finance it, we might buy it."

And to quote a friend: "There is always a buyer who thinks your lemon is his lemonade."

In summary, then, no small private company would be able to do the complex financing that is generally required in an LBO, unless the buyer is very wealthy and would pledge his own assets. Confidentiality in a small company is primary. If an announcement were made that a privately held company was for sale, and that all bidders were welcome, pandemonium would break out. The best employees would probably start to send out their resumes, the competitors' salespersons would probably start bad-mouthing the company, and the suppliers would get nervous. Soon there might not be much of a company left to sell.

In addition to that, small, privately held companies generally do not bring the high prices that LBOs bring. Because of the inherent risks in LBO financing, investors must foresee substantial rewards at the time of cash-out, five or seven years down the road. The rewards for transactions involving smaller companies may not be worth the risks. Thus it is unrealistic for an owner of a small company to expect the high multiples that the public-market companies are bringing. The big transactions are really auction sales involving the top 10% of large companies, where many of the lenders are looking for equity interest.

3

Traditional but Unacceptable Methods of Pricing a Business

I've never seen two deals alike, so there are no pat answers.

One of the most important things I have learned in the past ten years is that you can't trust the experts.

If everybody believes in the tooth fairy, then that's reality.

THIS book teaches you about how experienced, sophisticated, professional, rational buyers would examine a company for sale and the methods they would use to set a walk-away price, the highest price they might be willing to pay before they would walk away from the deal. (They would surely try to buy it for less during the negotiation.)

In this chapter we examine some of the traditional methods used to price a business, but methods that are inappropriate and unacceptable for pricing companies of the sort we are discussing in this book. You need to know about these methods so that you will be able to recognize them. Such knowledge may help you understand someone's basis for arriving at a price.

The primary methods we discuss here are:

- The IRS, or Treasury, method
- The discounted cash-flow method
- The net present-value method

We also present some additional tools to avoid: inappropriate estimation methods, rules of thumb, and formulas used in pricing various businesses.

IRS (or Treasury) Method

Uninformed sellers often set a price for their company based on the IRS, or Treasury, method. These valuation techniques are established by the U.S. government to set the value of a business when estate or gift tax forms must be filed. Values are determined by regulations, rulings, and legal precedent. While these methods work well in situations involving estates or gifts, they are inappropriate to use as a basis for setting a price in negotiation between a living buyer and a living seller in a free marketplace.

Prior to 1920, most companies were sold for the value of the physical, tangible assets. No extra value was given for *goodwill* (also known as "blue sky" or "key" money), which is the value of a business in excess of the physical assets. In 1920, the IRS issued ruling ARM 34, with formulas for valuing a business for estate and gift tax purposes. This ruling also established a formula for valuing goodwill, Later, other rulings were established, the most important being numbers 59-60 and 68-609.

Under the rulings, four techniques must be considered in the valuation:

1. Dividend capitalization
2. Book value and adjusted book value
3. Earnings, using comparable-price methods and capitalized earnings
4. Formulas method for adding goodwill based on excess profits

I have seen a cover letter, issued to a law firm by an accounting firm, with the following statement: "Valuation prepared in accordance with procedures in Revenue Ruling 59-60 and 68-609 is intended to provide a value for federal estate tax purposes and is to be submitted to the Internal Revenue Services." Remember, however, that the lawyers for the taxpayer and the IRS are adversaries. The estate lawyers would like a low figure, while the IRS would like a high figure to maximize the tax.

Here is a brief presentation of how each of the four techniques works.

Dividend Capitalization

To determine valuation based on dividend capitalization, assume that 40% of company earnings is paid for dividends (the balance of the earnings goes into the retained-earnings account). Next, determine the industry yield rate from the public market, that is, what other companies in your industry are paying. For example, if 5% is the dividend rate, then the value of the company is 20 times the amount paid for dividends (5% being 1/20th of 100).

For example:

A. If 40% of earnings is generally paid out in dividends, and if 40% of earnings is $20,000, and
B. If the industry average dividend yield is 5% of the market price, then

    C. Valuation based on dividend capitalizations = $400,000
       (i.e., 20 × $20,000)

Book Value and Adjusted Book Value

To determine valuation based on book value, start with the balance sheet. Keep in mind that this document is meant to support tax reports and does not necessarily reflect the market value of the assets. An adjusted book value at market price must be prepared, *without intangibles*. It would include:

    Cash
    Accounts receivable
    Inventory (add in reserves)
    Machinery and equipment, at current going-concern value,
       in place and debugged (by appraisal)
    Real estate, based on current appraisal
    Less liabilities and debt (omit goodwill and deferred taxes)

Capitalized Earnings

There are two ways to determine valuation based on earnings: the comparable-price method, and what is generally referred to as the "earnings method number 2."

Comparable Price Method

The first method uses the public market as a guide to establish value for a privately held company. For example, accountants determine the pretax income for the subject company as a percentage of equity for a five-year period. Once armed with five years of statistics, they compare those percentages with the percentages for a group of public companies with the same SIC code.

Next, they assign a mandated (by the IRS) weighted average to those percentages, applying weights of 1 through 5 to each year, with less weight for the most recent years. For example, assume the following five-year history of pretax income as a percentage of equity for the group of public companies with the same SIC code:

Weight Factor

1991:	14% ×	5 =	70	
1992:	13% ×	4 =	52	
1993:	12% ×	3 =	36	
1994:	11% ×	2 =	22	
1995:	10% ×	1 =	10	
Total		15	190	

$$\frac{190}{15} = 12.6\%$$

Thus, assume that a selling company's pretax earnings are $400,000. If capitalized at 12.6%, the value of the company would be $3,174,603.

Earnings Method Number 2

The second method to determine valuation based on earnings compares the price/earnings ratio (P/E) of the subject company with those in the public market.

The following example uses after-tax figures for both the public companies and the subject company. The assumption is that the subject company can be valued on the same basis as a group of publicly held companies with the same SIC number.

Assume that the industry group of public companies has a P/E of 12. Recognizing that private companies do not have the same marketability of shares as do public companies, the courts allow a discount for lack of marketability. Thus, if we use a discount factor of 40%, the theoretical equivalent of the industry P/E of 12 is 7.2 [12 × (1.00 − .40)]. For example, if the earnings per share are $20, and we multiply 20 times the P/E of 7.2, the value per share is $144.

If there are 10,000 shares, the value of the company is 10,000 shares times $144 per share, or $1,440,000.

Formula Method Ruling 68-609

The fourth technique for determining valuation is based on calculating excess earnings. According to IRS ruling 68-609, this requires a calculation where the value of the company is the sum of:

A. Tangible net worth (tangible assets less debt), plus
B. Intangible assets (goodwill, or the capitalized value of the excess earnings)

Let us take an example. Assume that a company has the following net worth and earnings:

A. Tangible net worth (tangible assets less debt)	$1,500,000
B. Average earnings after tax	$ 180,000
C. The ruling states that for tangible assets, the industry average should be used; where not available, an 8% or 10% rate of return may be used. If we use 10%, then 10% of $1,500,000 =	$ 150,000
D. Excess attributable to intangible assets (B minus C), or $180,000 less $150,000 =	$ 30,000
E. The regulation also states that the average earnings attributable to the intangibles should be capitalized at 15–20% (15% on small risks and 20% on higher risks). The multiplier on 15% is 6.67, and on 20% it is 5. In this example, if we use the 20% rate, the goodwill is 5 times $30,000, or	$ 150,000

The value of the company is the total of

tangible net worth	$1,500,000
goodwill	$ 150,000
Total Value	$1,650,000

In conclusion, these four IRS methods show values for tangibles and intangibles. However, buyers are not interested in intangibles as a separate value. The value of intangibles should be reflected in earnings after the deal is done, and negotiated as such. That is, intangibles become an element for the purpose of allocating assets.

*   *   *   *   *

There are people who use the rationale of the Treasury
methods to set a price for the company. I have seen many valuations based on a modified formula of capitalizing the earnings
at 20% (times five) with no normalization of the financials.
However, professional buyers would never accept such a rationale as a basis for reasonable price.

A more in-depth presentation of the Treasury methods is
contained in Report number 49, *Federal Estate and Gift Tax Reports, IRS Appellate Conferee Valuation Training Program*. It is
available from the Commerce Clearing House, 4025 W. Peterson
Ave., Chicago, IL 60646.

Discounted Cash Flow

The second unacceptable pricing method uses the discounted
cash flow. In fact, it is used by most appraisal companies' analysts or CPAs. However, for businesses and companies with
sales revenues of $1.5–30 million, the discounted cash-flow
method is not appropriate.

In order for this technique to be used effectively by buyer
and/or seller, a targeted company would need to have an
equivalent of a strategic planning group and rather sophisticated forecasting techniques. The assumptions that have to be
made are too exotic for smaller companies. In my experience,
none of the buyers I work with use the discounted cash-flow
technique as a basis for establishing a reasonable walk-away
price. But because it is referred to so frequently it deserves a
full discussion.

The theory behind the discounted cash-flow method is that
a company is worth the present value of its future earnings potential. In the early stage of negotiating for a company, experienced buyers have real estate, machinery, and equipment
appraised at market value; but they do not use the values developed by the appraisal firms for the purpose of setting their purchase price.

To establish the cash flow, determine the normalized after-
tax earnings and add back the depreciation. In Chapter 5, I ex-
plain how to arrive at a normalized figure. In essence, it means
that I adjust the profit and loss statement to add back into the
earnings any "excesses" that would not have occurred if simply

a professional, nonowner manager had been running the company, and if the purpose (of the privately held company) had not been to minimize taxes. For example, we would use a market price value for the manager's salary to reflect the "normal" earnings for the company.

The first thing to be done is to calculate the true cash flow for the last three years, as if the company had been professionally managed with no excesses. Then incorporate the assumptions that follow from that notion, such as asking what the earnings will be under a new owner, or under new management.

Here are some of the questions to be answered:

- What has the rate of growth in sales and earnings been over the last three years? (See Chapter 4 for the correct method of determining growth rate.) How much is attributable to inflation and how much to expansion?
- What are the assumptions about the rate of growth? Will it exceed the historical rate?
- Are the new owners smarter? Do they have better marketing strategies or the latest technology?
- Will the expansion require a new kind of organization or require new levels of management?

Buyers generally do not want to pay premiums for potential. For example, suppose a company has had a 12% growth rate over the last three years, and the buyer is presented with a study showing that the seller is sitting on a business about to explode to 18% or 20% growth per year. Most buyers will want to delve into the reasons for that optimistic projection. They need to be convinced of its validity.

According to the discounted cash-flow theory, the value of a company is the present value of its future earnings potential over a period of time, plus the present value of what will be the terminal value of net worth at the end of the three-year period. An example of a present-value calculation is shown in Exhibit 3-1.

When a discounted cash-flow statement is used as a basis for setting a price for a company in the $1.5–30 million size, the selling price ends up unreasonably high. Consequently the

Exhibit 3-1. Present-value calculation.

Assumption: estimated net worth at end of three years $2.6 million

End of year #	After-tax estimated cash flow (est. growth)	Future value of $1 at 15% discount	Present value
1	$1,000,000	.87	$ 870,000
2	$1,320,000	.76	$1,003,200
3	$1,520,000	.65	$ 988,800
Present value of cash flows			$2,861,200

Plus: present value of terminal value of $2.6 million in three years.
Assume a discount rate of 15%, which gives a factor of .65 from the present value table (Exhibit 3-2)   1,690,000

Present value of the company $4,551,200

company does not sell and instead becomes a stale commodity. The market simply says it is too high a price.

Sometimes the projections are totally unrealistic. For example, a company may have had a record of consistent earnings and steady, slow growth. In the last three years, it has had normalized cash flow totaling $2 million. Then an outside valuator, using discounted cash flows, projects cash flow for the next three years of $10 million under new ownership. Why? Most buyers will not accept that a new owner could accomplish such a feat while the current, experienced seller was not able to do so.

Net Present Value

Sophisticated buyers know their objectives and criteria. They understand that the money to pay back their investment—equity and debt—comes from the cash flow. And they understand the time value of money, that is, compounding for future value and discounting for present value.

For example, $1 invested at 10% compound interest will be worth $1.33 in three years.

Conversely, if you want to receive $1 in three years and if the interest rate is to be 10%, you need to invest $.75 now. In other words, $.75 is the net present value of $1 to be received in three years when the interest rate is 10%.

To put the necessary conclusion very simply, $1 in the hand today is worth *more* than $1 to be given to you three years from now.

Net present value is part of discounted cash-flow analysis. It involves the present value of future returns of cash flows. The returns can be in constant amounts, or they can vary from year to year.

Using the Net Present Value Tables

You have two basic decisions to make before choosing to use net present value tables:

   1. What is the time horizon? Over many years do you want to extend your payments or receipts?

2. What is the discount-of-interest-rate factor? That is, what is the minimum return or investment you want?

A buyer needs to consider three elements in making net present value calculations:

1. What will the cash flow be for each year into the future, until the cash flows have paid back the initial equity and debt paid for the company?
2. What is a reasonable estimate of the value of the original assets remaining at the end of the period?
3. Lastly, what adjustments, if any, need to be made for the long-term debt, and for any other liabilities incurred and still owed from the time the new buyer took over?

So all the buyer needs is these three elements: the present value of the cash flows, the residual assets, and the remaining liabilities.

Before we look at an example, let us discuss the two easy-to-read tables presented in Exhibits 3-2 and 3-3. You can get from the tables essentially the same results you would if you used a computer or a high-grade hand calculator programmed to do net present value problems.

Present Value of $1

The best way to understand Exhibit 3-2, the table for present value of $1, is to think about compound interest backwards.

For example, if you deposited $1 in the bank for five years at 8% with compound interest, it would be worth $1.47 at the end of five years.

Conversely, suppose someone promises you $1 in five years (in a single payment). If the person deposits $.68 at 8% interest, it will grow to $1 in five years. Exhibit 3-2 tells you how much that dollar in the future is worth today. Simply look at the exhibit, run your finger down to the row for five years, and then run your finger over to the 8% column to get the correct factor: 0.681. Multiply $1 times 0.681 and voilà!—the answer is $.68. That is, if that someone deposits $.68 today at 8% interest, in five years it will be worth $1. When you know the

Exhibit 3-2. Present value of $1.

This table shows the present value of one dollar received n years hence at i annual rate of return on the original investment. For example, to find the amount that would have to be invested today (the "present value") to receive $1 ten years hence if the annual rate of return earned was 10 percent, follow these steps: First, go across the top of the table to the 10 percent column. Next, go down this column until the ten years line is reached. The factor 0.386 is found at this location in the table. This factor indicates that an investment of approximately 38 cents today at 10 percent annual interest will grow to $1 in ten years.

Years Hence	1%	2%	4%	6%	8%	10%	12%	14%	15%	16%	18%	20%	22%	24%	25%	26%	28%	30%	35%	40%	45%	50%
1	0.990	0.980	0.962	0.943	0.926	0.909	0.893	0.877	0.870	0.862	0.847	0.833	0.820	0.806	0.800	0.794	0.781	0.769	0.741	0.714	0.690	0.667
2	0.980	0.961	0.925	0.890	0.857	0.826	0.797	0.769	0.756	0.743	0.718	0.694	0.672	0.650	0.640	0.630	0.610	0.592	0.549	0.510	0.476	0.444
3	0.971	0.942	0.889	0.840	0.794	0.751	0.712	0.675	0.658	0.641	0.609	0.579	0.551	0.524	0.512	0.500	0.477	0.455	0.406	0.364	0.328	0.296
4	0.961	0.924	0.855	0.792	0.735	0.683	0.636	0.592	0.572	0.552	0.516	0.482	0.451	0.423	0.410	0.397	0.373	0.350	0.301	0.260	0.226	0.198
5	0.951	0.906	0.822	0.747	0.681	0.621	0.567	0.519	0.497	0.476	0.437	0.402	0.370	0.341	0.328	0.315	0.291	0.269	0.223	0.186	0.156	0.132
6	0.942	0.888	0.790	0.705	0.630	0.564	0.507	0.456	0.432	0.410	0.370	0.335	0.303	0.275	0.262	0.250	0.227	0.207	0.165	0.133	0.108	0.088
7	0.933	0.871	0.760	0.665	0.583	0.513	0.452	0.400	0.376	0.354	0.314	0.279	0.249	0.222	0.210	0.198	0.178	0.159	0.122	0.095	0.074	0.059
8	0.923	0.853	0.731	0.627	0.540	0.467	0.404	0.351	0.327	0.305	0.266	0.233	0.204	0.179	0.168	0.157	0.139	0.123	0.091	0.068	0.051	0.039
9	0.914	0.837	0.703	0.592	0.500	0.424	0.361	0.308	0.284	0.263	0.225	0.194	0.167	0.144	0.134	0.125	0.108	0.094	0.067	0.038	0.035	0.026
10	0.905	0.820	0.676	0.558	0.463	0.386	0.322	0.270	0.247	0.227	0.191	0.162	0.137	0.116	0.107	0.099	0.085	0.073	0.050	0.035	0.024	0.017
11	0.896	0.804	0.650	0.527	0.429	0.350	0.287	0.237	0.215	0.195	0.162	0.135	0.112	0.094	0.086	0.079	0.066	0.056	0.037	0.025	0.017	0.012
12	0.887	0.788	0.625	0.497	0.397	0.319	0.257	0.208	0.187	0.168	0.137	0.112	0.092	0.076	0.069	0.062	0.052	0.043	0.027	0.018	0.012	0.008
13	0.879	0.773	0.601	0.469	0.368	0.290	0.229	0.182	0.163	0.145	0.116	0.093	0.075	0.061	0.055	0.050	0.040	0.033	0.020	0.013	0.008	0.005
14	0.870	0.758	0.577	0.442	0.340	0.263	0.205	0.160	0.141	0.125	0.099	0.078	0.062	0.049	0.044	0.039	0.032	0.025	0.015	0.009	0.006	0.003
15	0.861	0.743	0.555	0.417	0.315	0.239	0.183	0.140	0.123	0.108	0.084	0.065	0.051	0.040	0.035	0.031	0.025	0.020	0.011	0.006	0.004	0.002
16	0.853	0.728	0.534	0.394	0.292	0.218	0.163	0.123	0.107	0.093	0.071	0.054	0.042	0.032	0.028	0.025	0.019	0.015	0.006	0.005	0.003	0.002
17	0.844	0.714	0.513	0.371	0.270	0.198	0.146	0.108	0.093	0.080	0.060	0.045	0.034	0.026	0.023	0.020	0.015	0.012	0.005	0.003	0.002	0.001
18	0.836	0.700	0.494	0.350	0.250	0.180	0.130	0.095	0.081	0.069	0.051	0.038	0.028	0.021	0.018	0.016	0.012	0.009	0.003	0.002	0.001	0.001
19	0.828	0.686	0.475	0.331	0.232	0.164	0.116	0.083	0.070	0.060	0.043	0.031	0.023	0.017	0.014	0.012	0.009	0.007	0.003	0.002	0.001	
20	0.820	0.673	0.456	0.312	0.215	0.149	0.104	0.073	0.061	0.051	0.037	0.026	0.019	0.014	0.012	0.010	0.007	0.005	0.002	0.001	0.001	
21	0.811	0.660	0.439	0.294	0.199	0.135	0.093	0.064	0.053	0.044	0.031	0.022	0.015	0.011	0.009	0.008	0.006	0.004	0.002	0.001		
22	0.803	0.647	0.422	0.278	0.184	0.123	0.083	0.056	0.046	0.038	0.026	0.018	0.013	0.009	0.007	0.006	0.004	0.003	0.001	0.001		
23	0.795	0.634	0.406	0.262	0.170	0.112	0.074	0.049	0.040	0.033	0.022	0.015	0.010	0.007	0.006	0.005	0.003	0.002	0.001			
24	0.788	0.622	0.390	0.247	0.158	0.102	0.066	0.043	0.035	0.028	0.019	0.013	0.008	0.006	0.005	0.004	0.003	0.002	0.001			
25	0.780	0.610	0.375	0.233	0.146	0.092	0.059	0.038	0.030	0.024	0.016	0.010	0.007	0.005	0.004	0.003	0.002	0.001	0.001			
26	0.772	0.598	0.361	0.220	0.135	0.084	0.053	0.033	0.026	0.021	0.014	0.009	0.006	0.004	0.003	0.002	0.002	0.001	0.001			
27	0.764	0.586	0.347	0.207	0.125	0.076	0.047	0.029	0.023	0.018	0.011	0.007	0.005	0.003	0.002	0.002	0.001	0.001				
28	0.757	0.574	0.333	0.195	0.116	0.069	0.042	0.026	0.020	0.016	0.010	0.006	0.004	0.002	0.002	0.002	0.001	0.001				
29	0.749	0.563	0.321	0.185	0.107	0.063	0.037	0.022	0.017	0.014	0.008	0.005	0.003	0.002	0.002	0.001	0.001	0.001				
30	0.742	0.552	0.308	0.174	0.099	0.057	0.033	0.020	0.015	0.012	0.007	0.004	0.003	0.002	0.001	0.001	0.001	0.001				
40	0.672	0.453	0.208	0.097	0.046	0.022	0.011	0.005	0.004	0.003	0.001	0.001										
50	0.608	0.372	0.141	0.054	0.021	0.009	0.003	0.001	0.001	0.001												

Source: From tables computed by Jerome Bracken and Charles J. Christenson. Copyright © 1961 by the President and Fellows of Harvard College. Reprinted by permission of the Harvard Business School from David F. Hawkins, Corporate Financial Reporting: Text and Cases (Homewood, IL: Richard D. Irwin, Inc., 1977).

Exhibit 3-3. Present value of $1 received annually for n years.

This table shows the present value of $1 received annually for each of the next n years if i annual rate of return is earned on the remaining balance of the original investment throughout this period. For example, to find the amount needed to be invested today to receive $1 for each of the next 20 years if 10 percent can be earned on the investment, follow these steps: First, go across the top of the table to the 10 percent column. Next, go down the column to the 20 years line. The factor 8.514 is shown at this spot. This factor tells us that a 10 percent investment of $8.51 today will return to the investor $1 for each of the next 20 years. At the end of that time the investor will have recovered all of his original investment plus a return of 10 percent. Therefore, the present value of $1 per year for 20 years discounted at 10 percent is $8.51.

Years (N)	1%	2%	4%	6%	8%	10%	12%	14%	15%	16%	18%	20%	22%	24%	25%	26%	28%	30%	35%	40%	45%	50%
1	0.990	0.980	0.962	0.943	0.926	0.909	0.893	0.877	0.870	0.862	0.847	0.833	0.820	0.806	0.800	0.794	0.781	0.769	0.741	0.714	0.690	0.667
2	1.970	1.942	1.886	1.833	1.783	1.736	1.690	1.647	1.626	1.605	1.566	1.528	1.492	1.457	1.440	1.424	1.392	1.361	1.289	1.224	1.165	1.111
3	2.941	2.884	2.775	2.673	2.577	2.487	2.402	2.322	2.283	2.246	2.174	2.106	2.042	1.981	1.952	1.923	1.868	1.816	1.696	1.589	1.493	1.407
4	3.902	3.808	3.630	3.465	3.312	3.170	3.037	2.914	2.855	2.798	2.690	2.589	2.494	2.404	2.362	2.320	2.241	2.166	1.997	1.849	1.720	1.605
5	4.853	4.713	4.452	4.212	3.993	3.791	3.605	3.433	3.352	3.274	3.127	2.991	2.864	2.745	2.689	2.635	2.532	2.436	2.220	2.035	1.876	1.737
6	5.795	5.601	5.242	4.917	4.623	4.355	4.111	3.889	3.784	3.685	3.498	3.326	3.167	3.020	2.951	2.885	2.759	2.643	2.385	2.168	1.983	1.824
7	6.728	6.472	6.002	5.582	5.206	4.868	4.564	4.288	4.160	4.039	3.812	3.605	3.416	3.242	3.161	3.083	2.937	2.802	2.508	2.263	2.057	1.883
8	7.652	7.325	6.733	6.210	5.747	5.335	4.968	4.619	4.487	4.344	4.078	3.837	3.619	3.421	3.329	3.241	3.076	2.925	2.598	2.331	2.108	1.922
9	8.566	8.162	7.435	6.802	6.247	5.759	5.328	4.946	4.772	4.607	4.303	4.031	3.786	3.566	3.463	3.366	3.184	3.019	2.665	2.379	2.144	1.948
10	9.471	8.983	8.111	7.360	6.710	6.145	5.650	5.216	5.019	4.833	4.494	4.192	3.923	3.682	3.571	3.465	3.269	3.092	2.715	2.414	2.168	1.954
11	10.368	9.787	8.760	7.887	7.139	6.495	5.937	5.453	5.234	5.029	4.656	4.327	4.035	3.776	3.656	3.544	3.335	3.147	2.752	2.438	2.185	1.977
12	11.255	10.575	9.385	8.384	7.536	6.814	6.194	5.660	5.421	5.197	4.793	4.439	4.127	3.851	3.725	3.606	3.387	3.190	2.779	2.456	2.196	1.985
13	12.134	11.343	9.986	8.853	7.904	7.103	6.424	5.842	5.583	5.342	4.910	4.533	4.203	3.912	3.780	3.656	3.427	3.223	2.799	2.468	2.204	1.990
14	13.004	12.106	10.563	9.295	8.244	7.367	6.628	6.002	5.724	5.468	5.008	4.611	4.265	3.962	3.824	3.695	3.459	3.249	2.814	2.477	2.210	1.993
15	13.865	12.849	11.118	9.712	8.559	7.606	6.811	6.142	5.847	5.575	5.092	4.675	4.315	4.001	3.859	3.726	3.483	3.268	2.825	2.484	2.214	1.995
16	14.718	13.578	11.652	10.106	8.851	7.824	6.974	6.265	5.954	5.669	5.162	4.730	4.357	4.033	3.887	3.751	3.503	3.283	2.834	2.489	2.216	1.997
17	15.562	14.292	12.166	10.477	9.122	8.022	7.120	6.373	6.047	5.749	5.222	4.775	4.391	4.059	3.910	3.771	3.518	3.295	2.840	2.492	2.218	1.998
18	16.398	14.992	12.659	10.828	9.372	8.201	7.250	6.467	6.128	5.818	5.273	4.812	4.419	4.080	3.928	3.786	3.529	3.304	2.844	2.494	2.219	1.999
19	17.226	15.678	13.134	11.158	9.604	8.365	7.366	6.550	6.198	5.877	5.316	4.844	4.442	4.097	3.942	3.799	3.539	3.311	2.848	2.496	2.220	1.999
20	18.046	16.351	13.590	11.470	9.818	8.514	7.469	6.623	6.259	5.929	5.353	4.870	4.460	4.110	3.954	3.808	3.546	3.316	2.850	2.497	2.221	1.999
21	18.857	17.011	14.029	11.764	10.017	8.649	7.562	6.687	6.312	5.973	5.384	4.891	4.476	4.121	3.963	3.816	3.551	3.320	2.852	2.498	2.221	2.000
22	19.660	17.658	14.451	12.042	10.201	8.772	7.645	6.743	6.359	6.011	5.410	4.909	4.488	4.130	3.970	3.822	3.556	3.323	2.853	2.498	2.222	2.000
23	20.456	18.292	14.857	12.303	10.371	8.883	7.718	6.792	6.399	6.044	5.432	4.925	4.499	4.137	3.976	3.827	3.559	3.325	2.854	2.499	2.222	2.000
24	21.243	18.914	15.247	12.550	10.529	8.985	7.784	6.835	6.434	6.073	5.451	4.937	4.507	4.143	3.981	3.831	3.562	3.327	2.855	2.499	2.222	2.000
25	22.023	19.523	15.622	12.783	10.675	9.077	7.843	6.873	6.464	6.097	5.467	4.948	4.514	4.147	3.985	3.834	3.564	3.329	2.856	2.499	2.222	2.000
26	22.795	20.121	15.983	13.003	10.810	9.161	7.896	6.906	6.491	6.118	5.480	4.956	4.520	4.151	3.988	3.837	3.566	3.330	2.856	2.500	2.222	2.000
27	23.560	20.707	16.330	13.211	10.935	9.237	7.943	6.935	6.514	6.136	5.492	4.964	4.524	4.154	3.990	3.839	3.567	3.331	2.856	2.500	2.222	2.000
28	24.316	21.181	16.663	13.406	11.051	9.307	7.984	6.961	6.534	6.152	5.502	4.970	4.528	4.157	3.992	3.840	3.568	3.331	2.857	2.500	2.222	2.000
29	25.066	21.844	16.984	13.591	11.158	9.370	8.022	6.983	6.551	6.166	5.510	4.975	4.531	4.159	3.994	3.841	3.569	3.332	2.857	2.500	2.222	2.000
30	25.808	22.396	17.292	13.765	11.258	9.427	8.055	7.003	6.566	6.177	5.517	4.979	4.534	4.160	3.995	3.842	3.569	3.332	2.857	2.500	2.222	2.000
40	32.835	27.355	19.793	15.046	11.925	9.779	8.244	7.105	6.642	6.234	5.548	4.997	4.544	4.166	3.999	3.846	3.571	3.333	2.857	2.500	2.222	2.000
50	39.196	31.424	21.482	15.762	12.234	9.915	8.304	7.133	6.661	6.246	5.554	4.999	4.545	4.167	4.000	3.846	3.571	3.333	2.857	2.500	2.222	2.000

Source: From tables computed by Jerome Bracken and Charles J. Christenson. Copyright © 1961 by the President and Fellows of Harvard College. Reprinted by permission of the Harvard Business School from David F. Hawkins, Corporate Financial Reporting: Text and Cases (Homewood, IL: Richard D. Irwin, Inc., 1977).

time period, and when you know the interest rate, net present value is a simple process.

Present Value of $1 Received Annually for n Years

Exhibit 3-3 is a table for determining the present value of $1 received for *n* years. It is used where payments are to be made annually over a period of years, that is, where you want to know the present value that will produce a given series of payments. For example, if you promise to pay someone $50,000 a year for five years, that will equal $250,000. Depositing $180,250 at 12% today allows you to pay $50,000 a year for five years, while you earn 12% on the remaining balance.

In Exhibit 3-3, run your finger down to the row for five years, and then across to 12%. The factor is 3.605. Multiply this factor times the annual payment:

$$\$50,000 \times 3.605 = \$180,250$$

Here is how it looks, showing the calculations for each of the five years:

	Beginning Balance	Amount of Interest @ 12%	Total	Less Annual Payment	Year-End Balance
End of Year 1	$180,250	+$21,630	$201,680	$50,000	$151,880
End of Year 2	$151,880	+$18,226	$170,106	$50,000	$120,105
End of Year 3	$120,105	+$14,413	$134,518	$50,000	$84,518
End of Year 4	$84,518	+$10,142	$94,660	$50,000	$44,660
End of Year 5	$44,660	+$5,359	$50,019	$50,000	$19

Thus, $180,250 deposited for five years at 12% earns enough interest to allow you to make annual payments of $50,000 (and have $19 left over).

Valuation Using Discounted Cash Flow

The following scenario illustrates valuations using the discounted cash flow method.

Assume 10% growth per year for the next five years. The

buyer's calculation of the maximum price might look something like Exhibit 3-4. (Note: In this example, where the annual cash flow is not constant but varies each year, we use only Exhibit 3-2.)

The increased value in this scenario is attributable to the annual growth in earnings.

Valuation Using Net Present Value

The following scenario illustrates valuations using the net present value method.

Assume a company with constant earnings (no growth) over a five-year period. The buyer requires a 12% return after tax. The calculation of the buyer's walk-away price might look like this:

A.	Net income for 1995	$50,000
B.	Add depreciation	20,000
C.	Adjusted cash flow	$70,000
D.	Present value discounted at 12% for five years. See Exhibit 3-3, to obtain factor of 3.605. Multiply the annual cash flow (line C) times the factor:	
	$\times$ 3.605	$252,350
	Less the long-term debt	$-$ 62,350
E.		$190,000
F.	Estimated value of the noncash assets as of 12/31/00 (accounts receivable, inventory, fixtures):	$75,000
G.	Less liabilities 12/31/2000	$-$ 25,000
H.	Present value of the assets	$50,000
I.	See Exhibit 3-2 to locate the present value factor for 12% for five years: 0.567 Multiply 0.567 times $50,000 (line H):	$+$ $28,350
J.	The total estimated walk-away price for a company with a cash flow of $70,000 a year for five years, and a residual value of the assets of $50,000 where the inventor wants to earn 12% after tax (lines E plus I):	$218,350

Exhibit 3-4. Buyers' calculation of maximum price (at 10% growth per year for next five years).

	Last Day of Prior Year	End of Year 1	End of Year 2	End of Year 3	End of Year 4	End of Year 5
A. Net income	$50,000	$55,000	$60,500	$66,550	$73,200	$80,520
B. Add depreciation	20,000	20,000	19,000	18,000	17,000	16,000
C. Adjusted cash flow		$75,000	$79,500	$84,550	$90,200	$96,520
D. Line c multiplied by the present value factor (12%) for five years (see Exhibit 3-2)	× .893	× .797	× .712	× .636	× .567	
E. Present value of the cash flow		$66,975	+ $63,361	+ $60,199	+ $57,367	+ $54,726 =
F. Sum of values on line E						$302,682
G. Less adjustment for long-term debt Original balance of 12/31/95		$62,350				
Reduced on 12/31/2000		$50,000			$252,682	
H. Present value on noncash assets					+ $75,000	
I. Less liabilities on 12/31/2000 remaining from 12/31/95 (if any)					− 25,000	
					$50,000	
J. Multiply line I times present value factor (12% for five years) (see Exhibit 3-2) 56.7 × $50,000 =						$ 28,350
K. Valuation using discounted cash flow: maximum price (G + J)						$281,032

Additional Inappropriate Methods

Be prepared to reject a price if a seller bases it on any of the following rationales.

Ratio of Invested Capital to Cash Flow Using a Multiplier

While the ratio of invested capital to cash flow is used by some public companies to establish a price, it is inappropriate to compare prices of public companies with private companies. Even the courts cannot agree how much to discount public company ratios and discounts, because there is no ready stock market for private companies.

Let us make the following assumptions for a debt-free company:

Assumptions:

1. Equity:		$600,000
2. Long-term debt:		$200,000
Interest @ 10% rate = $20,000		
3. After-tax earnings:	$90,000	
4. Depreciation:	+ 30,000	
5. Cash flow:	$120,000	
6. Add back estimated 40% tax (federal and state) on $20,000 interest		+ 8,000
7. Debt-free cash flow:		$128,000
8. Divide equity (1) plus the long-term debt (2) by debt-free cash flow; ($600,000 + $200,000) ÷ $128,000		= 6.25 (ratio)
9. Do research on a group of public companies in your industry, and work up the same formula for the public companies as in step 8. Assume the answer is a ratio of 6.17. You would then use 6.17 as		

the multiplier of your debt-free
cash flow (step 7):

$128,000 × 6.17 =	$789,760
10. Deduct the long-term debt	200,000
11. Value of the company	$589,760

Multiple of Net Worth

If a seller bases the selling price on after-tax earnings or a multi-ple of net worth, reject it. Professional buyers do not base sell-ing price on after-tax earnings because many adjustments need to be made to the operating earnings in order to show the pro-spective buyer what the earnings before taxes are.

Price as a multiple of net worth, based on after-tax earn-ings as a percent of sales, is another method not used by profes-sional buyers.

Here is how the formula works:
If after-tax earnings represent 3% of sales, the value = one times net worth

@ 5% = two times net worth
@ 7% = three times net worth
@ 9% = four times net worth
@ 11% = five times net worth

Valuation Using Goodwill

If a seller bases the selling price on a formula using goodwill, a buyer should reject it. To the professional buyer, goodwill is used only as an accounting term to show the difference be-tween the value of the tangible assets and the purchase price. This following is a modification of methods used by lawyers to determine a value for estate purposes.

Here is an example of how the goodwill formula would be used. Assume:

A. Tangible net worth	$300,000
B. Estimated equivalent return on alternative investment such as CDs, bonds = 10%	$30,000
C. Salary and benefits for manager with no ownership interest	$72,000

D. Earnings pretax, and presalary $120,000

E. Goodwill/excess earnings calculation

Pretax earnings (D) $120,000
      minus (B)   30,000
      minus (C) $ 72,000

F. Excess earnings $ 18,000

G. 3 years' excess earnings (F)
$18,000 × 3 $54,000

H. Value of company
Tangible net worth (A) + three years'
excess earnings (G)
$300,000 + $54,000 = $354,000

About Formulas and Rules of Thumb

The final section in this chapter deals with formulas and rules of thumb that are not acceptable methods of pricing for professional buyers. I have never been involved in the sale of a company or business where the price was based on a formula, nor do I know any buyers who would work up a value for a company they are interested in based on an industry formula. However, formulas and rules of thumb are used in some transactions. For example, some small stores are sold at prices set by formula, as are some very large service companies, such as insurance agencies and fuel distribution companies. Sellers often base their expectations, too, on some formula. We need to know what these formulas are and how they are used.

The formulas are generally derived from any of the following:

1. The use of a multiplier of gross sales, to which are added values of inventory, accounts receivable, or real estate
2. The use of a multiplier based on earnings
3. The use of a multiplier based on the number of units, such as the number of rooms in a motel

Because they offer ways of setting a price, here are some of the formulas and rules of thumb that a variety of different businesses might use to arrive at a selling price. *Caveat emptor.*

You should simply be aware of these formulas as you try to figure out how a seller has come up with an asking price. These formulas and rules of thumb are *not* being presented as guidelines for your use.

Here is a list of different types of businesses and the formulas that some sellers might use to arrive at a selling price. All of the information that follows is based on personal communications and on general industry practice.

> *Telemarketing company:* 9–12 months' fees
> *Collection agency:* 3–5 months' fees for cash collected
> *Telecommunications company:* 6–10 months' fees
> *Golf course—if not owned by members, if near population centers where housing is not permitted, or if not in a flood plain:* 7–10 times cash flow
> *Discount chain—high-fashion, ready-to-wear retailers:* about one-half of annual revenues
> *Media production company:* 2 or $2^1/_2$ times annual gross revenues
> *Corporate shell with a loss carryforward:* generally 20% of the loss
> *Accounting practice:* 100–150% of gross annual billings, with no participation in increased fees, and paid on retained accounts over three years
> *Weekly paper:* 12 months' gross volume
> *Bakery:* 10 times the weekly gross
> *Power washing company:* 3 times the cash flow
> *Motel:* $3^1/_2$ times the gross room revenues for one year (before local taxes). Resort areas sell for 5 times annual gross room revenues. The numbers will work to handle expenses and debt service.
> *Liquor store in Connecticut:* inventory plus $30,000 for each $100,000 of sales. This pays for goodwill, fixtures, office. The only extra might be for recent purchases of refrigeration. The owners' benefit will be about 9% of sales. One point to note about inventory: Many times the inventory value exceeds the 50% down payment figure. Sellers don't want to deliver more inventory than covered by the down payment. Many times it is possible for the seller to withdraw excess inventory from the original

sale, and then sell it to the buyer as needed and have it paid off over time.

Pizza place in Florida: 2 times annual earnings, pretax, pre-owner's benefits. Food cost should not exceed one-third of revenues. One recent buyer sat at the cash register for two weeks and scrutinized outside delivery orders to make sure they were not fictitious. He had passed on an opportunity to buy another pizza place after examining the purchases and discovering that the owner had borrowed receipts from a friendly competitor to show higher sales.

Insurance agency: generally one year's commission to be paid over a three-to-five-year basis on retained customers

Oil distributor: generally sold for the value of the assets, plus a multiple of the gallonage. If the mark-up is $.09 a gallon, then the seller might collect $.03 per gallon per year for three years on retained accounts. If the mark-up is $.21, then the payment might be $.07 per gallon per year for three years on retained customers.

Bodega in the New York area: selling price of $10,000 for each $1,000 of weekly sales

Supermarket: inventory plus value of one month's sales

Coca-Cola franchise: $10 times number of cases sold annually

Country store: tangible assets plus 175% of owners' benefits, consisting of salary, profits, health insurance, car, etc.

Beer distributor: physical assets plus $1.50 per case sold annually

Laundromat: $1 of sales price per $1 of revenue for one year. Can adjust up or down for location, decent lease, and whether the equipment will have to be replaced during the next five years.

Personal care line: when purchasing a trademark, formulations, and market information, but no plant and no facilities. If the line could realize 16% on sales, the buyer would pay $1 for each dollar of sales. If 30% on sales, the buyer would pay $2 for each dollar of sales.

Cable TV: 11 times cash flow

Ad agency: 75% of annual gross income

Day care center: $500 to $1,000 per child

Dry cleaner: 60% of annual volume

Drug store: 40% of gross sales, or 100 days' sales

Garbage route: 2 to $2^1/2$ times gross income for year

Mom-n-pop store (cash-type Main Street store): determine the seller's discretionary income, that is, how much the owner takes out of the business in one form or another. The rule of thumb is 2 to $2^1/2$ times the discretionary income. The price includes inventory and equipment. Generally sold with one-third down payment, and payout not to exceed the length of the lease.

Brothel: When the Mustang Ranch in Nevada was sold, the enterprise had 108 bedrooms. The gross receipts were $5.3 million, with earnings of $917,000. The asking price was $25 million, and it finally sold for $18 million. That works out to $166,666 per room.

Health and beauty aids: If the pretax earnings are 16%, pay $2 for $1 of sales.

Brick yard: also $1 for each $2 of sales

Many small cash-flow businesses use rules of thumb for valuations. For example, it is common to hear that one pays six months' sales for a tavern, or 40% of gross sales for a restaurant, or seven months' sales for a franchise, or five months' sales for a round-the-clock fast-food place.

The following are some more generalizations frequently heard about very small enterprises (under $300,000 in sales):

Generalization 1

Many times, these small companies sell with about 50% down payment plus the cost of inventory or supplies. The seller finances the 50% balance for anywhere from three to 10 years. There are some brokers who will not take a listing unless the seller agrees to do the financing.

Generalization 2

Normally, the buyer can expect to do about $2 to $3 in sales annually for each $1 of the purchase price. Example: A buyer paying $50,000 for the business can expect to do about $150,000 in sales.

Generalization 3

With 30% down, for every $1 of down payment equity a buyer will earn from $1.50 to $2.50 pretax, before draw or salary for himself, and before payback to the seller.

Generalization 4

The above ratios apply to food or drink enterprises. For a service company involving equipment, such as a laundromat, the purchase price will be equal to the amount of the annual sales, but the return on the down payment will still be about $1.50 of earnings for $1 of down payment. For example: assume $50,000 in sales at the laundromat. Then the enterprise will sell for about $50,000, with about $18,000 down; it should earn about $27,000 pretax, pre-payback, and pre-draw.

Generalization 5

Businesses with inventory have some rules of thumb that are commonly repeated. They vary with stock turnover, the spread between retail price and cost of goods, markup, and type of business. For example, a small market will sell for about two months' sales plus inventory. Assume a market with annual sales of about $200,000 (average of $16,700 a month) and inventory of $20,000. It will probably sell for about $53,000 ($33,000 plus the inventory). A typical down payment might be $30,000.

Generalization 6

Service companies sell for about one year's earnings plus tangible assets.

Generalization 7

The small entrepreneur is generally satisfied if he can take in enough dollars to provide a "living," with some perks, payback of the debt, and payment of taxes.

Generalization 8

The key to selling small, cash-type stores is seller financing, with 50% down payment. The seller must realize that the tax return is what is for sale—and that there is very little financing available from the banks.

The problem with rules of thumb is that you must still use other methods to determine whether the numbers work. Questions to be asked in determining that the numbers work include:

> Will there still be enough positive cash flow to pay the manager, to pay off the debt service, and to pay the taxes?
> What does that leave for the new owner?
> What are the earnings of the company, if any?
> What are the values of the assets transferred?

The sales volume alone does not tell whether the operation is profitable. The figures do not tell you whether the revenue is going up or down, and what the local economic environment is now and in the near future.

A final comment: When knowledgeable people are asked, "How much can I get for my business?" they usually answer, "It depends."

4

Capital
Budgeting
Techniques

When you're carrying lots of debt, pray that your projections work out.

An unrealized gain is the same as an unrealized loss.
—*Stanley Pratt*

I don't mind a price that is a little high, so long as it is not wild. I like to see a price with a shred of rationality.
—*Roy Bonwick*

BEFORE we get to Chapter 5, which discusses EBIT pricing, we need to examine additional terminology. We have already dealt with discounted cash flow in Chapter three. In this chapter, we take up the following topics:

- How to calculate return on equity (ROE) properly
- How to calculate compound growth properly
- How to calculate the internal rate of return, or discounted rate of return
- How to calculate the return of *net* operating assets
- How to calculate the payback period
- Some notions about cash flow
- How bankers look at a company

How to Calculate Return on Equity

The one important ratio we look at is the return on equity (ROE), also called return on net worth. How much did the company earn either pretax or after-tax as a percentage of year-end equity? Most people calculate these significant figures incorrectly by dividing earnings by the equity at year end.

For example, if this year's year-end earnings are $304 and equity is $1,852, one might be tempted to divide 304 by 1,852 to get 16.4%. That method is wrong. The proper method is to take the *average* for the past two years (end of the last year plus end of this year, divided by two).

The correct method follows:

Average of year-end equity this year	= $1,852
Average of year-end equity last year	= 1,686
	$3,538
Divide by 2	= $1,769

Then divide this year's earnings by the average equity:

$$\frac{304}{1,769} = 17.2\%$$

17.2% is the return on net worth, or return on equity.

How to Calculate Return on Investment

Return on investment (ROI) is not the same as return on equity. Your investment is the purchase price, made up of your equity plus the long-term debt needed to finance the company's purchase—that amount which you are responsible for repaying. The formula to determine the return on investment is:

$$\frac{\text{Earnings}}{\text{Equity plus the long-term debt on which you pay interest}}$$

Using the above example:

$$\frac{\$304}{\$1852 + \$597} = \frac{\$304}{\$2449} = 12.4\%$$

Suppose your company is for sale and the buyer wants a 20% return on investment. That means he is willing to pay five years' earnings. Suppose your after-tax earnings for the last five years were as follows:

1995	$400,000
1994	$335,000
1993	$225,000
1992	$150,000
1991	$100,000

Do not be too fast in concluding that you can expect five times $400,000, or $2 million. A sophisticated buyer might want to use a weighted average on the earnings, giving the greatest weights to the most recent years. Weights of 1 through 5 would be applied to each year, 1 to the earnings of five years ago, and 2 to the earnings of four years ago, and so on.

		Weight factor	
1995	400,000 ×	5 =	2,000,000
1994	335,000 ×	4 =	1,340,000
1993	225,000 ×	3 =	675,000
1992	150,000 ×	2 =	300,000
1991	100,000 ×	1 =	100,000
	1,210,000 ×	15 =	4,415,000

$294,333 is the weighted average earnings ($4,415,000 divided by 15).

$242,000 would be the unweighted average earnings over the last five years ($1,210,000 divided by 5).

$400,000 is the last year's earnings.

As the seller, you might be valuing, arguing, and negotiating from the $400,000 figure. In general, a sophisticated buyer looks at the $294,333 figure (although she might be negotiating from the nonweighted average figure of $242,000). The buyer's final offer might be $294,333 × 5 years = $1,471,665—not the $2 million you were expecting based on 1995 earnings.

In many very small companies, the buyer is generally looking for 20% minimum return. That 20% has to include owner's salary and benefits, earnings, and tax shelters.

If a seller can demonstrate higher ROI, say 25% or 30% instead of 20%, a buyer will probably pay a higher price for the company. The ROI must be in excess of the cost of capital, whether equity or debt; otherwise the buyer will have no benefit. Leverage (borrowing) lowers the percentage of return, but it allows the buyer to make additional investments.

According to data from the New York Stock Exchange, most of the top earners in each industry make at least 15% after taxes. That is after depreciation, big salaries, 30–35% fringe benefits on wages, and R & D expenses.

One final thought on ROI:

If a company is bought for $1 (equity and debt)
and produces $2 of sales
and earns after tax $.20
it earns 20% ROI.

How to Calculate Compound Growth Rates

In general, the reason a buyer wants to know about the growth rate is to compare your company with the industry and the economy. The buyer wants to know whether earnings are flat, or average for industry growth, or reflecting super growth. Sustained super growth, of course, means having to pay a premium. In fact, as long as the company's growth rate is greater than the industry growth rate, the seller usually looks for a premium.

According to Baron Rothschild, compound interest is the eighth wonder of the world. However, calculating compound interest is a fairly simple exercise. This may well be familiar to you, but here is a quick review of how to calculate growth rates.

Say, for example, that a company had sales five years ago of $1 million. If sales this year are $2 million, then we can say that sales have doubled in five years, and doubling means a 100% increase. But doubling in five years is not a 20% annual growth rate, as you might guess. Instead, we are dealing with a *compounded* rate. In the case of doubling in five years, the growth rate is about 15% per year, as shown below:

Example of 15% Compounded Rate

End of year 1:	$1,000,000 + 15% (150,000) = $1,150,000
End of year 2:	$1,150,000 + 15% (172,500) = $1,322,500
End of year 3:	$1,322,500 + 15% (198,375) = $1,520,875
End of year 4:	$1,520,875 + 15% (228,131) = $1,749,006
End of year 5:	$1,749,006 + 15% (262,350) = $2,011,356
	(or about $2 million)

A growth rate of 20% would result in sales of about $2.5 million in 5 years, as follows:

Example of 20% Compounded Rate

End of year 1:	$1,000,000 + 20% (200,000) = $1,200,000
End of year 2:	$1,200,000 + 20% (240,000) = $1,440,000
End of year 3:	$1,440,000 + 20% (288,000) = $1,728,000
End of year 4:	$1,728,000 + 20% (345,600) = $2,073,600
End of year 5:	$2,073,600 + 20% (414,720) = $2,488,320
	(about $2.5 million)

Calculating the compounded growth rate using a table is even simpler.

For example, assume an increase in sales (or earnings) from $1 million to $2 million in a five-year period. Divide the final-year number ($2 million) by the first-year number ($1 million) to arrive at a factor, in this case 2. Then, using the compound growth rate chart (Exhibit 4-1), go down the left-side column to year 5. Then move to the right until you reach the figure closest to 2, which is the factor. Then move up to the top

Exhibit 4-1. Compound growth rates.

Years	1%	2%	3%	4%	5%	6%	7%	8%	9%
1	2.010	1.020	1.030	1.040	1.050	1.060	1.070	1.080	1.090
2	1.020	1.040	1.061	1.082	1.103	1.124	1.145	1.166	1.188
3	1.030	1.061	1.093	1.125	1.158	1.191	1.225	1.260	1.295
4	1.041	1.082	1.126	1.170	1.216	1.263	1.311	1.361	1.412
5	1.051	1.104	1.159	1.217	1.276	1.338	1.403	1.469	1.539
6	1.062	1.126	1.194	1.266	1.340	1.419	1.501	1.587	1.677
7	1.072	1.149	1.230	1.316	1.407	1.504	1.606	1.714	1.828
8	1.083	1.172	1.267	1.369	1.478	1.594	1.718	1.851	1.993
9	1.093	1.195	1.305	1.423	1.551	1.690	1.839	1.999	2.172
10	1.105	1.219	1.344	1.480	1.629	1.791	1.967	2.159	2.367

Years	10%	12%	14%	15%	16%	18%	20%	24%	28%
1	1.100	1.120	1.140	1.150	1.160	1.180	1.200	1.240	1.280
2	1.210	1.254	1.400	1.323	1.346	1.392	1.440	1.538	1.638
3	1.331	1.405	1.482	1.521	1.561	1.643	1.728	1.907	2.097
4	1.464	1.574	1.689	1.749	1.811	1.939	2.074	2.354	2.684
5	1.611	1.762	1.925	2.011	2.100	2.288	2.488	2.932	3.436
6	1.772	1.974	2.195	2.313	2.436	2.700	2.986	3.635	4.398
7	1.949	2.211	2.502	2.660	2.826	3.186	3.583	4.508	5.630
8	2.144	2.477	2.853	3.059	3.278	3.759	4.300	5.590	7.206
9	2.358	2.773	3.252	3.518	3.803	4.436	5.160	6.931	9.223
10	2.594	3.106	3.707	4.046	4.411	5.234	6.192	8.594	11.805

of that column, where you find the compound rate. In this case, the number closest to 2 is 2.011, and the figure at the top is 15%.

If the factor were 2.5, the compound growth rate would be 20%; if the factor were 1.2, the compound growth rate would be 4%.

The Internal Rate of Return

The internal rate of return (IRR), also known as the discounted rate of return, equates the present value of the future cash flows (earnings and depreciation) with the purchase price. In a sense, it is a way of measuring a kind of return on investment over a period of time. The answer is given as a percentage.

The IRR measures whether a company is growing or shrinking in value. If the IRR exceeds the cost of capital, the company will grow. If the IRR is less than the cost of capital, the value of the company will shrink.

For example, if the capital cost is 10%, and the IRR is 10%, the company will neither shrink nor grow.

If the capital cost is 10% and the IRR exceeds 10%, the company will grow.

If the capital cost is 10% and the IRR is less than 10%, the company will shrink in value.

We need the following information to solve for the IRR:

1. What is the cost of capital?
2. What is the amount of the original investment, equity, and debt?
3. A prediction about the annual cash flows (earnings and depreciation).
4. The residual value—what the company will be worth in X years.

The assumed values are:

1. The investment
2. The predicted cash flows
3. The estimate of the residual

The unknown is the internal rate of return. This is what we want to solve for, to determine whether the IRR will exceed the cost of capital.

Cost of Capital

To find the cost of capital, we have to calculate the cost of the equity portion and the debt portion. For example, assume that someone buys a company for $100,000. Assume the buyer has equity of $40,000 and borrows debt of $60,000 at 10%. Also assume that the buyer is looking for a 12% return on investment (if he cannot make the 12%, he will not do a deal).

Here is how to calculate the cost of capital: The equity of $40,000 is 40% of the investment. Multiply the percentage of the equity times the desired return:

$$40\% \text{ of } 100,000 \times 12\% = 4.8\%$$

The debt of $60,000 is 60% of the investment. Multiply the percentage of the debt times the desired return:

$$60\% \text{ of } 100,000 \times 10\% = 6.0\%$$

Cost of capital = 4.8% plus 6.0%, or 10.8%

Now that we know how to find the cost of capital, let us set up two examples to find the IRR.

The easiest way to solve such problems is with a hand calculator that can do IRR problems. However, if you do not have a hand calculator, you can use the Present Value of $1 chart (Exhibit 3-2). Granted, this is a cumbersome trial-and-error method in which you have to go from one column to another, and do your calculations until the sum of the present values of the cash flows and the cash flow of the residual almost match the amount of the investment. It can be done, but only by experimentation.

Example 1

Let us make the following assumptions:

1. The cost of capital is 10%.
2. The proposed purchase price is $750,000.
3. The cash flows for the next few years will be $195,000 each year.

4. The $750,000 company will still have a residual value of $750,000 after three years.

The solution to Example 1 is given in Exhibit 4-2.

Example 2

Let us make the following assumptions:

1. Cost of capital 10.8%.
2. Purchase price of $400,000.
3. Cash flow as follows:
   At end of year 1 $24,000
   At end of year 2 $26,000
   At end of year 3 $28,000
   At end of year 4 $30,000
4. Residual value at the end of either year three or year four will still be $400,000.

The solution to Example 2 is given in Exhibit 4-3.

Hurdle Rates

Some sophisticated companies use a combination of both the cost of capital and the IRR to set a target number for making a favorable assessment of a possible acquisition. (Sometimes these companies will tell you what that number is, and sometimes they will not.) That certain number or rate is often called the *hurdle rate*. Different companies use different rates. It is a way of adding the cost of capital to the growth-expectation rate.

For example, a company might say that they require a hurdle rate of 22.8%, made up of both equity and debt cost:

Cost of capital	10.8%
Plus the IRR	12.0%
Equals hurdle rate	22.8%

Return on Net Operating Assets

Return on net operating assets is an approach used by some large, sophisticated companies to establish the value of a smaller company they are interested in buying.

For example, the buyer might have acquisition criteria indicating that any investment must have a return of 20% on the net operating assets.

The formula is simple. The return on net operating assets equals:

$$\frac{\text{Net earnings}}{\text{Net operating assets}}$$

Assume that the value of the net operating assets is $600,000. (The net assets include, for example, enough cash for operations, the inventory, the receivables, and fixed assets less depreciation. Any excess cash or outside investments or securities are deleted.)

The calculation for net earnings is earnings less taxes. Using sample figures:

Pretax earnings	$200,000
Less income tax	88,000
Net earnings (after tax)	$112,000

If the hurdle rate for the buyer is 20%, the above company would not be purchased at $600,000—unless at a discount, or unless the seller could show the buyer how the return on net operating assets could be increased to 20%.

Most entrepreneurs are not interested in this method to establish a price. Most entrepreneurs only want to know two things:

How much am I putting in?
How much am I making on what I put in?

We discuss this method here primarily because if you are dealing with a large public company you should be familiar with this approach. They might be using it.

Another way a company might describe a subsidiary is as follows:

Sales	$18 million
Investment	6,120,000

(text continues on page 89)

Exhibit 4-2. Worksheet for Example 1: $750,000 investment with even annual earnings of $195,000 per year.

Trial-and-error method: First try to solve at different rates until you come up with two that are close to the proposed purchase price. In this example, starting with 20% gives you $843,975, which is not very close to $750,000. Trying again with 24% and 28% gets you closer to the desired number.

	After-tax cash flows	Present value factor A	Extension 20%	Present value factor B	Extension 24%	Present value factor C	Extension 28%
Year 1	$195,000	.833	$162,435	.8065	$157,170	.781	$152,295
Year 2	195,000	.694	135,330	.6504	126,750	.610	118,950
Year 3	195,000	.578	112,710	.5245	102,180	.476	92,820
Year 3	750,000	.578	433,500	.5245	393,000	.476	357,000
			$843,975		$779,000		$721,000
			not close		closer to 750,000		closer to 750,000

We can see that the internal rate of return is between 24% (column B) and 28% (column C). By interpolation, we can solve for the correct rate. Here is the formula:

First: Original investment minus the lesser of the sums closer (C) divided by the higher of the sums closer (B) minus the lesser of the sums closer (C) times the difference between the higher rate (B) minus the lower rate (C)

Thus:

$$\frac{750,000 - 721,000}{779,000 - 721,000} \times (28\% - 24\%)$$

$$= \frac{29,000}{58,000} \times 4\%$$

$$= .5 \times 4\% = 2\%$$

Now *add* this answer to the lower of the two interest rates:

$$2\% + 24\% = 26\% \text{ IRR}$$

This is a roundabout way of getting the answer. The much easier way is to use a calculator. Incidentally, given a cost of capital of 10% and an IRR of 26% in this example, this is an outstanding investment.

Exhibit 4-3. Worksheet for Example 2: $400,000 investment with uneven annual earnings. (Residual value at the end of three years: still $400,000.)

At end of year	Total investment	After-tax cash flows	Present value factor @ 6%	Extension	Present value factor @ 8%	Extension
0	($400,000)		0	0	0	0
1		$24,000	.943	$22,632	.926	$22,224
2		26,000	.890	23,140	.857	22,282
3		28,000	.840	23,520	.794	22,232
4		430,000	.792	340,560	.735	316,050
	($400,000)	$508,000		$409,852		$382,788

Note: The total of the present values at 6% is $409,852, which is just a little higher than the original investment of $400,000. The total of the present values at 8% is 382,788, just a little lower than the original investment of $400,000. So we can say that the IRR is between 6% and 8%, certainly less than the 10.8% cost of capital. This company would be shrinking and would not be an attractive purchase.

Return on sales after corporate charges and after taxes	4.5%

How to Calculate the Payback Period

Payback period is easy to understand. It does not measure profitability, it does not reflect the time value of money, and it is not concerned with the value of the assets after the payback. It refers to a period of time: how many years it will take to recover the original investment from the cash flow.

If you invest $100,000 to purchase a company and your annual after-tax earnings are $25,000, your original investment is paid back to you in four years.

$$\frac{\text{Investment}}{\text{Annual after-tax earnings}} = \frac{\$100,000}{\$25,000} = 4 \text{ years}$$

Many buyers of small companies use payback as a key element in their decision.

Some Notions About Cash Flow

There are many meanings of *cash flow*.

To some it answers the questions, "During which months of the year will I have enough money to pay my bills when due? And during which months will I have to borrow money to pay my bills?" Cash flow is a way of reviewing the cash in and the cash out.

To others it means "What am I getting out of my company? What am I getting in the form of cash payments currently, or in the form of deferred payments later? What fringes am I getting that I do not have to pay income taxes on? What benefits do I get that are taxable?"

To some, especially in leasing or in real estate, it is a way of calculating how much cash they can take out of an enterprise or an investment without paying taxes.

To others, it is a way of measuring how quickly they are collecting their accounts receivable.

And to a banker, it is a way of analyzing how you expect to repay your loan.

I use the term *cash flow* in this book to mean what funds are or will be available after taxes at the end of the year for future expansion, and for repayment of the debt.

The source of such funds is made up of the profit (or earnings) and depreciation. Why depreciation? Depreciation is treated as an expense, deducted from income but with no money paid out. It is only a matter of bookkeeping. The amount set aside for depreciation is a noncash expense and is available for distribution or for an increase in working capital.

Smart buyers know that money will also be needed for unexpected emergencies, and for expansion. Only a favorable cash flow provides the ability to expand. If there are no earnings, and if there is no cash, why would anyone want to buy the company?

How Bankers Look at a Company

Many investors feel that up to 50% of the after-tax cash flow should be available for debt servicing—payment plus interest. However, one banker I know prefers a 35% payout. He wants to make things easier, and not choke the buyer with high debt payments; he is willing therefore to extend the payout period. He knows that cash is needed for working capital, expenses, debt service, taxes, and to have a little cushion. You cannot pay bills with book income; you need cash.

Quick Tests

Bankers use two ''quick tests'' to get a reading on how efficient a company is. One measures the turnover rate for accounts receivable; the other measures inventory turnover.

Accounts Receivable Turnover

The quick test to measure how quickly the company collects its bills uses this formula:

$$\frac{\text{Annual sales}}{\text{Average accounts receivable}} = \frac{\$3,500,000}{\$\ \ 500,000} = 7$$

$$365 \text{ days} \div 7 = 52 \text{ days}$$

Most bankers would find that rate to be fast and current.

Inventory Turnover

Here is the formula for a quick test of a company's inventory turnover rate:

$$\frac{\text{Cost of goods sold}}{\text{Average inventory}} = \frac{\$2,440,000}{\$375,000} = 6.5$$

$$365 \text{ days} \div 6.5 = 56 \text{ days}$$

This would be an excellent turnover rate.

Financing Work-Up

Here is an example of a work-up by a banker to determine how to arrange the financing of a sale of a company, where the selling price is $3,250,000.

Fixed asset loan	$1,400,000 @ 80% =	$1,120,000
Accounts receivable loan	$ 400,000 @ 75% =	$ 300,000
Inventory loan	$ 410,000 @ 60% =	$ 246,000
Total loans on assets		$1,666,000
One-day loan (cash available in the company)		$ 500,000
Unsecured loan, to be paid from cash flow		$ 750,000
Cash from buyer, plus working capital		$ 334,000
		$3,250,000

5

Normalized EBIT Earnings and Earn-Outs

> I know how to value a company that is making money. I don't know how to value a company that is losing money.
>
> *—A successful investor*

> In the beginning, the seller said it had to be a cash deal, and that the buyer had to take over the real estate. In the end, he was taking paper and kept the real estate.

> Most sellers don't understand the sensitive relationship between price and earnings, and the fragility of value. If earnings are down, the value is down; and if earnings are up, the value is up.
>
> *—Roy Bonwick*

THIS IS VERY IMPORTANT ©

I N this chapter we discuss how successful professional buyers and sellers set a reasonable price, one that is competitive in the marketplace. This chapter presents the rationale for using EBIT earnings (earnings before interest and taxes) to arrive at a reasonable price.

We have already discussed the Treasury methods and explained that they are not acceptable methods for buying or selling a company. We have discussed the discounted cash-flow methods and explained why they are not suitable for companies of the size we are considering. We have discussed the LBO public market, and its influence on pricing smaller companies, and why it is not a suitable basis for establishing values and prices for privately held, smaller companies.

A friend recently had lunch with her banker. She and the banker were playing "what if." What if I wanted to sell the company; how much could I expect to sell it for? The banker said that with sales of $6 million and pretax normalized earnings of 15% on sales ($900,000), my friend could expect between $4 million and $6 million. The owner wanted to hear $6 million. The difference of $2 million is 33% of that target, which is too wide a range. It seems that a professional ought to be able to focus the target price in a narrower range, so the seller is able to have a sensible conversation with her accountant about tax consequences.

But even when the advice is more targeted, no one can predict with total accuracy what a buyer might be willing to pay. Let us recognize that in a group of sophisticated and qualified buyers, there will be variations about how much each will pay. Nevertheless, if they want to buy, they have to be competitive with the marketplace.

Most sellers have high expectations. But if they want to sell they, too, have to be in the ballpark of the marketplace. The collective wisdom of the marketplace develops a price from a combination of factors:

Supply and demand
Company financials
The economy
Negotiating skills
Good luck and bad luck
Salesmanship and enthusiasm on the part of both buyer and seller

The buyer must be able to see a clear presentation of the profitability of the selling company. The buyer must know whether the sales and earnings are flat or growing. If growing, by how much? The buyer also needs to know what operating assets (facilities, equipment, etc.) are required to produce the earnings.

In general, buyers are earnings buyers, not asset buyers. Everything is reflected in the earnings. If the seller wants to get a reasonable price for her company, she must do her home-work. She must normalize the financials to show a prospective buyer what the earnings of the company really are—as if the owner had treated the company without excesses—and what reasonable expenses would be at market prices. We know that the function of a publicly held company is to increase the wealth of the company. We know that a privately held company is run for the benefit of the owner, and that the financials are tax documents. So there is work to be done to have the normalized statements reflect a correct picture of a company's balance sheet and income statements for a purchaser. The price depends on the earnings, which support the price.

There must be a clear picture of what the true assets and liabilities are, and what the true earnings have been and where they are going. We define *true earnings* as earnings before interest and taxes, or *EBIT* earnings. For companies bought on an EBIT basis, this means that the walk-away price is established by adjusted earnings before interest and taxes, times a multiple established in the marketplace, less interest-bearing debt.

This method is used by knowledgeable investors, holding companies, buyers of businesses, lenders, banks who have moved beyond asset lending to cash-flow lending, sophisticated deal-making lawyers, and accountants. The marketplace has been the teacher. It is the current collective wisdom of the marketplace.

The kinds of companies I deal with, those with an inventory component, are generally bought on the basis of EBIT pricing if they *qualify* (that is, for example, if they have succession management in place). Disregard goodwill. Disregard the P/E of the public marketplace. Disregard the ratios of a company selling at a multiple of book value. Disregard the return-on-equity ratios compared with the public market. Also disregard the ratio of selling price as a percent of book value or as a multiple of P/E.

We must get to understand the real earnings from the perspective of a buyer—as if the company were operated by a non-stockholder professional manager.

What the Experts Say About EBIT Pricing

The following quotes about EBIT pricing are from active and successful buyers (individual and corporate). They show that most experts believe in and practice EBIT pricing.

Company 1:

EBIT is the standard formula for determining sales price for a business. We pay extra for super growth.

Company 2:

We are pure EBIT buyers. We are not too concerned about assets or blue sky (goodwill). Our range is five to seven EBIT. Our concern is how to pay the debt and cut into sales, general, and administrative charges.

Company 3:

Our company will pay 10 to 12 times after tax [equals 5.6 pretax] for a company with 10% to 12% after-tax ROI. We are concerned with constant earnings. The value is reflected in normalized earnings. We buy management and confidence in the management.

Company 4:

We require a minimum of $5 million in earnings. We will pay eight times pretax earnings, but the company must have market leadership, or superior growth, or at least 25% growth in earnings for the next three years.

Company 5:

Will pay five to six EBIT for companies with 15% to 20% ROI. The price range depends on the growth rate and profit rate.

Company 6:

Most of our deals are cash-flow deals. What can the company finance? Five to six EBIT is what we can pay with a 3-to-1 debt-to-equity ratio.

Company 7:

If there are no earnings, we cannot buy on multiples.

Company 8:

We will pay five EBIT, if we can get 12% after tax on our investment [equal to 20% pretax at combined 40% tax rate].

Company 9:

When the adjusted book value of tangibles is less than 50%, we will pay pretax EBIT.

Company 10:

We will not pay over five times EBIT where the net worth of tangibles is not at least 60% of the selling price (unless they have a special franchise, a valuable patent, or special permit).

Company 11:

We will pay up to five EBIT on the high side plus a component for excess working capital.

Company 12:

We are EBDIT buyers. [*EBDIT* is a variation of EBIT; it stands for earnings before depreciation, interest, and taxes.] So depreciation is added back, just like interest and taxes. We will pay seven to eight EBDIT, when:

(1). Earnings are a minimum of $4 million
(2). After-tax returns of net assets are in excess of 15%, using the formula

$$\frac{\text{net income}}{\text{net producing assets}}$$

(made up of net working capital, plus fixed assets, plus other assets)

(3). There is in-depth management.

Company 13:

We pay for extraordinary growth, that is, above 15%. We want 25–30% pretax with 15% growth. Twenty percent would be extraordinary. We would expect to pay down 50% of the debt in five years and then exit.

Company 14:

We will pay four to six EBIT if there are prospects for growth, and there is no requirement for new capital.

Company 15:

We will not pay six EBIT for any company with sales under $25 million.

Company 16:

We will pay up to $5^{1}/_{2}$ EBIT provided the IRR (internal rate of return) is 25%.

Company 17:

We pay five EBIT on a $10 million company, with $1–3,000,000 of our own. On a $1 million company we will pay four or five EBIT. The smaller the company, the more fragile our investment is with a one-man show.

Company 18:

Regarding the influence of growth on the EBIT multiple, we will pay eight EBIT for a company that can grow 25% per year over the next three years.

Company 19:

We will buy companies with a minimum EBIT of $1.5 million and pay four to five EBIT, but the company must have:

(1). Historical stability of earnings (no glitches)
(2). Quality of management, or very strong middle management
(3). Opportunity for growth

We are not interested in day-by-day involvement of operations. We can help with controls and strategic planning, and provide capital for future growth.

Company 20:

We have gone from four EBIT and now are paying five to six. At six we require good growth, strong market position, and a good product. At six we need earnings increases and growth above average.

Company 21:

We need $2 million in operating profit. We will pay four to $4^1/_2$ EBIT less interest-bearing debt (trade payables not factored in).

Company 22:

We will pay six to seven EBIT, but only if there will be an increase in earnings.

Company 23:

We look at multiples of adjusted book value:

(1). If book value is less than one-half of selling price, we will pay $4^1/_2$ to five EBIT.
(2). If book value is higher than half of selling price, we will pay five to six times.
(3). We require minimum earnings of $2 million.

How to Do the EBIT Work-Up

Before the seller can set a reasonable price, he or she must answer the following question: "What is it that is for sale?"

- Is it to be a stock sale for 100% of the stock? For 100% of the balance sheet? Or for something else?
- Will some of the assets be withdrawn before the sale, such as cars, boats, planes, campsites, condominiums, securities, nonoperational assets? If so, what would the balance sheet look like?
- Would the interest-bearing debt and capital-lease obligations be assumed by the buyer? Or will the debt be paid before the transfer?
- Will there be adequate net working capital on the transfer? Or will an infusion of more money be required?
- Is it to be an asset sale for a debt-free company? For all of the assets? Or for some of the assets?

The seller should know what the tax consequences will be under either type of sale (stock or asset), and also what the tax consequences will be for the buyer.

To begin the work-up, the first thing to be done is to normalize (some people would say to adjust to economic value, to recast, or to rebuild) the balance sheet and the P&L. We have to

end up with the statements you would expect if a manager who had no ownership in the company were operating the company. We are looking for a statement from the perspective of a new owner who wants a true picture of the underlying assets and liabilities that were used and required to produce the earnings. In other words, "What are the true earnings of the company from ordinary and extraordinary operations?"

Let us assume that a stock sale is desired. The buyer and seller must know the current value of the tangible net worth (equity). The balance sheet is a tax document and an accounting document; it generally does not reflect current market values. Usually three areas on the balance sheet need special adjustment: real estate, machinery and equipment, and inventory.

Real Estate

A current appraisal is required for all real estate. In general, the buyer will need such an appraisal to get financing. It is a good idea for the seller to get an appraisal early, to support the rationale of the eventual price.

Machinery and Equipment

It is also a good idea to get an appraisal for machinery and equipment early on to support the rationale for the price. The appraiser generally provides three valuations. In a recent situation involving book value of $730,000, the appraiser provided the following assessment:

Auction value (if sold at auction within 60 days)	$1 million
Orderly liquidation value (if sold in an orderly manner within 12 months)	$1.5 million
Value in place (shipped, set up, and "debugged")	$2 million

For purposes of financing, bankers generally look at the first two values; for purposes of selling the company, the value-in-place figure is what the seller will be looking at. The appraisal does not tell anyone what is obsolete, what has to be replaced, what is prime, and what needs rebuilding. Make sure the valuation includes items that have been fully depreciated, as well as any tools, dies, jigs, and other elements needed to support the figure for machinery and equipment.

If items are leased, prepare a list of items under lease, to be able to show it to the buyer.

The buyer will ask for a facilities list along with the appraisal. Make sure it is presentable, clear, and businesslike.

Inventory

Most privately held companies will have to make additions to normalize the inventory, either because of previous write-offs, goods left over from contracts, or material left over from where inventory was supplied, or because year-end inventory was understated to reduce tax liability. Now it is time to pay back some of the taxes previously deferred.

In some companies, such as job shops, there is almost no inventory because it has been supplied by the original contractor. Where there is inventory, it must be brought to current market price for the raw material. Work in process will probably be figured at cost, and finished goods may or may not be figured with the profit. Be prepared to discuss with the buyer how the inventory was figured.

If the statements are not audited (and in most cases they will not be), the issue of unaudited inventory can become a trouble spot. In that case, talk to a good deal-making accountant to discuss how this problem can be alleviated. The issue of inventory valuation is very important to the buyer. It is a tool in arranging financing.

In retail and distributing companies, inventory is generally not complicated, because the way you buy it is the way you sell it. The buyer needs to have a sense of what the inventory is worth, what is obsolete, what is on consignment, what is out of fashion, and what is slow moving. Salable goods are generally figured at market or replacement cost. There are plenty of appraisers and inventory-takers available to help companies with inventories.

We have now learned how to bring the balance sheet to its current value, to know what the underlying assets and liabilities are, what the working capital is and how it is made up, and what the current value of the owner's equity is. An example of a normalized balance sheet is shown in Exhibit 5-1.

This has been part one of the exercise. We now go to part two, which is the work-up of the normalized EBIT.

The Normalized EBIT Work-Up

The work-up of the EBIT worksheet is the most important document required in the preparation of a sale. Without it, neither the buyer nor the seller has a basis for establishing a reasonable price, a price with a rationale. Until the buyer can see what the EBIT figures are, nothing of significance will happen. Nothing will move. With the EBIT worksheet, the seller has, for the first time, a clear understanding of what the benefits are and have been. By the same token, the buyer is given a picture of the true earnings, without which he or she cannot make a decision about buying or selling.

EBIT is the basis for the buyer and seller to have discussions with their lawyers, accountants, and tax advisers about price and alternatives.

The seller needs to make adjustments to the pretax earnings to show a buyer what the true earnings of the company would have been if there had been no excesses for the owner's benefit, and if the owner/manager had accepted a market price salary for working as a professional manager.

The owner's benefit can mean many things. Here are just three examples.

> An owner asked a friend to give his opinion on what he thought he could get for his company. In digging for information in order to arrive at an EBIT figure, the friend discovered that the company had 22 leased cars, of which five were used by family members who did not work for the company.

> In another case, an owner had his ex-wife on the payroll, even though she did not work for the company. This arrangement was in lieu of paying alimony.

> In a third situation, the owner confided to a colleague that his Florida office was really an apartment he

maintained for his father. All phone calls coming into the Florida number were rerouted to the main office in New Jersey. The father's sole job was to go to the post office daily to pick up the mail from a postal box, put it into a large envelope, and remail it to the New Jersey office.

Obviously, the value of these types of owner's benefits would have to be added back before true earnings could be calculated.

Some people are EBIT buyers and require a cash-flow figure. That means that we must add depreciation to the EBIT figure. Almost all professional buyers are EBIT buyers. Cash flow becomes an important issue when there is a factor of incremental fixed capital investment.

When developing a normalized EBIT worksheet, there are items to be added to or subtracted from the pretax income figure on the P&L. They include:

1. Extraordinary, nonrecurring abnormal, nonoperating, or nonbusiness expenses—such as moving expenses, litigation, conversion from FIFO to LIFO, fire losses, and theft—generally result in lower earnings and should be added back.
2. Inventory adjustment for reserves taken in prior years. Add it back.
3. Interest paid. Add it back.
4. Items for the owner's or owner's family's benefit. These are excesses. When the owner's salary is above market price, add back the entire amount of the owner's salary and make a deduction for an appropriate amount for a manager's salary. Also, add back all special expenses and fringes for the owner, including life insurance, owner's bonus, cars, legal counseling (personal), financial counseling (personal), medical, excess travel and entertainment, nonbusiness expenses involving hobbies, such as boats, vacation homes, and excess salaries. In other words, add back all those expenses that will disappear after the sale.
5. Payroll should be added back for nonworking members of the family, who will be off the payroll after a closing.

(text continues on page 110)

Exhibit 5-1. Balance sheet (in $000s).

	Book value	Omit	No adjust. required	Adjust entire amt. to fair market value +	Adjust entire amt. to fair market value −	Normalized market value
Current assets:						
A. Cash	$ 15,490		X			$ 15,490
B. Accounts receivable	29,716				$350	29,366
C. Inventory	52,788			$ 7,918		60,706
D. Prepaid expense	2,020		X			2,020
E. Current assets	$100,014					$107,582
Fixed assets:						
F. Land	$ 3,842			$11,602		$ 15,444
G. Buildings	19,608			20,200		39,808
H. Machinery & equip.	50,719			10,600		61,319
I. Furn. & fixtures	74,169					
J. Less depreciation	34,476					
K. Net Fixed assets	39,693					$116,571
L. Tangible assets	20,897					
M. Deferred charge	1,155		X			1,155
N. Total assets	161,759					$225,308

Current liabilities:			
O. Accounts payable	$ 19,099	X	$ 19,099
P. Short-term borrowing	11,606	X	11,606
Q. Taxes payable	1,919	X	1,919
R. Accrued expenses	2,481	X	2,482
	$ 35,106		$ 35,106
Long-term liabilities			
T. Long-term borrowing	$ 47,762	X	$ 47,762
U. Other liabilities	4,000	X	
			82,868
V. Equity	74,891		142,440
W. Liability & Equity	$161,759		$225,308

The same holds true for cars and other benefits for non-working members of the family, such as director's fees, noninterest loans, or charges for nonbusiness private projects.

6. Excess depreciation, prepaid expenses including advertising, co-op advertising, advertising to be reimbursed, and payments forthcoming.

7. Rental expenses should be at market price. If the rental is below market, adjust and subtract from income, unless there are long-term leases in effect. If the rent is above market and would be adjusted at the closing, the excess is to be added back into income.

8. If there are nonoperating assets that will not be transferred at closing, such as real estate in the company's name, any expenses incurred for those assets and paid by the company should be added back into income.

I have noted two frequently occurring items that are subtracted from income, namely, a deduction for a manager's salary and rental adjustment if the rent paid is above market price. Other adjustments need to be made when the company owns investment assets, such as stocks; bonds; and nonoperating, investment real estate. In those cases the calculations for EBIT must break out the interest received, dividends received, and rental income, and subtract them from income. At the same time, add back to income the expenses paid by the company related to these assets.

The EBIT figure must reflect the true operating earnings of the company. If the investment assets are not to be transferred, then it is proper to remove income and expenses on these items from the operating P&L. If these nonoperating assets are to be included in the sale, it is proper to develop a value for the operating assets of the company and add a component for these investment items to the EBIT figure.

Earn-Outs and Contingencies

Some time ago, the newspapers reported that the WPP Company had acquired a private company for $6.25 million cash and stock up front, with an additional $7.75 million potentially to be paid over time. The ultimate price would be based on a multiple of 10 times the after-tax earnings (about six times pretax) for a three-year period after the closing. Such a contingency payment is called an *earn-out*. If the anticipated earnings are achieved, the buyer will pay the seller the contingency when achieved.

One of our buyers states in his criteria that he prefers that any price in excess of net tangible assets be principally in earn-outs or notes payable out of earnings.

Another buyer reviewed an opportunity to buy a company. The seller wanted $7 million for the company, which was $2 million over the tangible net assets. The seller based the price on a forecast showing a large increase in sales and earnings. The current year's earnings were $1.5 million and the seller was projecting $1.8 million for the next year. The buyer agreed to buy the company with an earn-out, that is, to pay the price only if the forecast was achieved.

Earn-outs are a way of accommodating the different views of the buyer and the seller. The buyer will pay more money later, but only if projected earnings levels are realized.

A recent transaction involved a company for sale that was on the verge of exploding into new sales levels, and there was a difference of opinion on how big the explosion would be. The historical annual pretax earnings had been about $600,000. The sale proposal was for $2.5 million up front (which was about $1 million over the value of the tangibles) plus 20% of the pretax between $500,000 and $1 million, 30% between $1 million and $1.5 million, and 35% over $1.5 million, if realized. Thus, if for example the company's earnings reached $1.6 million, the total price would be $2,785,000. If earnings did not grow as predicted and remained at the $600,000 level, the price would be $2,520,000.

Buyers and sellers usually differ regarding the base to which the earn-out is pegged. Sellers generally want the earn-out pegged to sales, because that is easy to check. Buyers generally want the earn-out pegged to earnings. (It is hard to monitor an earnings earn-out, but not impossible.) Occasionally a deal may collapse because this issue cannot be resolved.

Sometimes earn-outs have a maximum ceiling for participation, and sometimes they do not. Sometimes an agreement may provide that no contingency will be triggered until 15% pretax has been achieved. Earn-outs are a way of maintaining a strong incentive for the seller to remain interested in the business and to stay on, either as an employee or as a consultant.

6

Normalized EBIT Pricing of Type A and Type B Companies

If a company doesn't have something special, don't overpay.

—*Ted Cohen*

Buying a company is easy. Financing a company is hard.

We liked the numbers. Now we want to see the people behind the numbers.

THERE are two basic EBIT pricing methods used to arrive at a reasonable price. To select a method, we can divide companies into two categories, type A and type B. Whichever category the seller fits into establishes which pricing method is used to price the company.

Pricing a Type A Company

The type A company is constantly profitable. It differs from a type B company in that it has management that depends on one or two people, with neither a strong management team nor a strong successor in place. It is without a special market niche.

A sale of this kind of company is generally an *asset sale*, not a stock sale, for the normalized net worth of the assets *plus* approximately one year's worth of owner's benefits.

If the real estate is owned by the seller, then adjust the income and expense as if the real estate were rented at market price. If the buyer wants the real estate, add it to the EBIT price.

When the earnings are extraordinary, or if there is a doubt as to the sustainability of earnings, then perhaps postclosing payments can be made in future years via earn-outs.

If there is no strong management, pricing is based on the net worth of the assets plus one year's EBIT, rather than on a multiple of the earnings. The buyer will want all or most of the people who are responsible for the past earnings to continue working in the company.

Here are some general points to remember:

1. Make an allowance for a nonowner manager's salary.
2. If growth has been over 15% (or is expected to be over 15% because of new products or something big about to happen), see the section on earn-outs in Chapter 5.
3. If the seller wants to take out most of the tangible net worth, such as cash, accounts receivable, and real property, and maybe just leave the machinery and equipment, furniture and fixtures, or inventory, then expect the price to be:

• The value of the assets (and expect deep negotiations about leasehold improvements)

- Plus about one year's normalized EBIT
- Minus any debt to be assumed

How to Prepare an EBIT Worksheet for a Type A Company

The EBIT worksheet is generally part of the long-form profile of the company, which is shown to buyers who have qualified as having a strong interest in the company and capacity to close. A blank EBIT worksheet is shown in Exhibit 6-1. The following notes refer to the handwritten numbers on the form in that exhibit.

#1. At this point, the name of the company and its location have not been identified, so all the references are to a file number.

#2. The first three blank columns show figures for the last three years. The fourth column is for a projection, if reasonable.

#3. Use net sales figure.

#4. Use pretax income from P&L.

#5. All the adjustments that will be added to and subtracted from the pretax to arrive at EBIT are listed in this section. Exhibit 6-2 lists examples of items that are normally part of these adjustments.

#6. This is the magic EBIT figure, without which nothing can move forward. It is the basis for arriving at a reasonable selling price, and at a walk-away price for the buyer. The buyer must know what the earnings are to support the selling price. Most buyers do not rely on projections; they want the facts.

#7. The EBIT percentage of sales for the years covered shows whether your performance is average, above, below, or exceptional, and whether it is so on a consistent or erratic basis.

#8. For those who are interested in the cash-flow figure, list the depreciation.

#9. EBIT with depreciation added becomes EBDIT.

#10 and #11: In order to understand what the underlying tangible assets are in the proposed transaction, (a) if it is an asset deal, just list the current market price of the tangible assets to be acquired; (b) if it is a stock deal, the buyer needs to know whether the normalized equity and the book value of tangible assets omit the value of all intangibles, including goodwill.

THIS IS VERY IMPORTANT ©

Exhibit 6-1. EBIT worksheet (re: File #1 in $000s).

Re: File # ①   in $000s.

Fiscal year ending ②	10/31/93 ③	10/31/94 ③	10/31/95 ③	PROJECTION 11/31/96
Sales				
Pretax from P&L			④	
Normalizing adjustments				
1.				
2.				
3.				
4.				
5.			⑤	
6.				
7.				
8.				
9.				
10.				
11. EBIT normalized			⑥	
12. EBIT as % of sales	%	%	% ⑦	%
13. + Depreciation			⑧	
14. = Cash flow (EBDIT)			⑨	

Comments:

From Balance Sheet

Date: _____

Net Book Value
(Omit all intangibles,
like goodwill) $ _____

Add Adjustments:
    Inventory reserve   _____

Real Estate:
    Appraisal   _____
Less:
    book value   _____

Other Fixed Assets:
    Appraisal   _____
Less:
    book value   _____

Other assets previously
depreciated or expensed*
*(list on reverse side)   _____

Normalized
Net Book Value Without Intangibles $ ⑩ AND ⑪

From Balance Sheet
Working Capital $ _____ ⑫

Current Portion of
Long-Term Debt $ _____ ⑬

Long-Term Debt $ _____ ⑭

Exhibit 6-2. Some examples of items that appear frequently in adjustments to the EBIT worksheet.

Re: File # _____ in $000s.

Fiscal year ending				
Sales				
Pretax from P&L				
Normalizing adjustments				
1. Interest paid				+
2. Owner's salary				+
3. Owner's perks, pension				+
4. Owner's profit sharing				+
5. Owner's insurances				
6. Rent adjustment (if above or below market)				+ or (−)
7. Nonrecurring loss of business; assume the % of pretax				+
8. New manager's salary				−
9.				
10.				
11. EBIT normalized				
12. EBIT as % of sales		%	%	%
13. + Depreciation				
14. = Cash flow (EBDIT)				

Comments:

#12. In a stock deal, there will probably be an agreement about how much the working capital must be as of the date of the transfer. This is a good place to establish whether the working capital is representative, with a surplus, or thin.

#13. Items such as demand notes and the current portion of the long-term debt are part of the current liability section. The buyer may or may not assume the debt, so he or she should have a clear picture of the working capital with and without the debt.

#14. If the long-term debt is to be assumed in a stock transaction by the buyer, it must be deducted from the selling price. The EBIT price is for a debt-free company.

Exhibits 6-3 and 6-4 show typical completed EBIT worksheets for type A companies. The owner of the company shown in Exhibit 6-3 planned to leave after the sale; the remaining management is very thin. A reasonable price for this company would be the value of the tangible assets ($1.4 million) plus one year's EBIT ($833,000), or about $2.2 million.

The owner and key managers of the company in Exhibit 6-4 also plan to leave after the sale. A reasonable price for this company would be about $1.2 million, based on assets of $900,000 and one year's EBIT of $317,000.

Pricing a Type B Company

The type B company is also a consistently profitable company, but it has a strong first and/or secondary management team that will remain after a sale.

Persons and companies who are regularly in the marketplace to buy type B companies use EBIT pricing. That is, they pay a multiple of the earnings, before interest and taxes, less interest-bearing debt to be assumed. The multiple is a function of competition, interest level, marketplace, and what is required to pay off and service the debt.

I did not invent this method. It is the standard method for the purchase of private companies in this range that have well-organized management teams, companies that, in addition to operations, have successful planning, marketing, and financial

(text continues on page 124)

Exhibit 6-3. Asset sale: type A company.

Re: File # B302 in $000s.

Fiscal year ending	2 yr. prior	1 yr. prior	Last year	Projection
Sales	3,900	4,200	5,600	
Pretax from P&L	140	198	145	
Normalizing adjustments				
1. Owner's salary/pension	529	635	738	
2. New manager's salary	(80)	(90)	(100)	
3. 2 extra cars	20	20	20	
4. Other perks	30	30	30	
5.				
6.				
7.				
8.				
9.				
10.				
11. EBIT normalized	639	793	833	
12. EBIT as % of sales	16%	19%	15%	%
13. + Depreciation				
14. = Cash flow (EBDIT)				

From Balance Sheet

Date: _____

Net Book Value
(Omit all intangibles,
like goodwill) $ _____

Add Adjustments:
Inventory reserve   _____

Real Estate:
Appraisal   _____
Less:
book value   _____

Other Fixed Assets:
Appraisal   _____
Less:
book value   _____

Other assets previously
depreciated or expensed*
*(list on reverse side)   _____

Normalized $1,400,000
Net Book Value Without Intangibles

From Balance Sheet
Working Capital $ _____

Current Portion of
Long-Term Debt $ _____

Long-Term Debt $ _____

Comments: Owner leaves shortly after sale.
Very thin management—tremendously successful, but a one-man show.
A reasonable price would be value of tangible assets, $1,400,000
                                        one year's EBIT   833,000
                                                                $2,200,000

Exhibit 6-4. Asset sale: type A company (another example).

Re: File # 2122 in $000s.

Fiscal year ending	2 yr. prior	1 yr. prior	Last year	Projection
Sales	1,900	2,050	2,220	
Pretax from P&L	161	206	223	
Normalizing adjustments				
1. Owner's salary	150	163	175	
2. New manager's salary	(80)	(80)	(85)	
3. Owner's perks	90	103	110	
4. Profit sharing	11	8	8	
5. Interest received	(30)	(24)	(24)	
6.				
7.				
8.				
9.				
10.				
11. EBIT normalized	232	293	317	
12. EBIT as % of sales	12%	14%	14%	%
13. + Depreciation	19	15	21	
14. = Cash flow (EBDIT)	251	308	338	

Comments: Asset sale—owner to leave, then management leaves.

A reasonable price

Assets	$ 900,000
one year's earnings	317,000
For a debt-free company	$1,217,000

From Balance Sheet

Date: _____

Net Book Value
(Omit all intangibles,
like goodwill) $320,000

Add Adjustments:
Inventory reserve   140,000

Real Estate:
Appraisal   _____
Less:
book value   _____

Other Fixed Assets:
Appraisal   540,000
Less:
book value   100,000   440,000

Other assets previously
depreciated or expensed*
*(list on reverse side)   _____

Normalized $900,000
Net Book Value Without Intangibles

From Balance Sheet
Working Capital $ _____

Current Portion of
Long-Term Debt $ _____

Long-Term Debt $ _____

capabilities. Generally, if companies cannot meet these criteria, they are sold as type A companies.

How to Set a Reasonable Market Price for a Type B Company

In this section, we consider some general guidelines for pricing a type B company, that is, one with consistent earnings, with professional management, and with planning, marketing, financial, and technological capabilities.

In recent years, the EBIT multiple has been inching up for larger companies where there is great demand.

Where the growth is under 15%, the price range will be $4^1/_2$ to $5^1/_2$ times EBIT, or five times EBIT plus or minus 10%. Take, for example, a company free of non-interest-bearing debt with $6.5 million in sales and with $900,000 of EBIT. The sales price would probably be between $4 million and $5 million ($4^1/_2$–$5^1/_2$ times $900,000). That means if the buyer is to assume the long-term debt, the debt is deducted from the EBIT multiple.

How the seller gets $5 million instead of $4 million is probably a combination of finding a buyer who thinks in terms of EBIT as well any of the following factors:

- Luck
- Supply and demand
- Timing
- Special niche in the market
- Special proprietary product
- Enthusiasm of the buyer and of the seller
- Negotiating skills
- Terms
- Chemistry of the buyer and seller
- Tax situation
- Asset sale versus stock sale
- What percentage of the sales price is goodwill
- What percentage is tangible assets

In a stock sale, sometimes the negotiation can be for the entire balance sheet. Sometimes it is for the operating assets, for the working capital and fixed assets, or for some other variation.

In a business with inventory (unlike a service business), the buyer will probably expect 50%–70% of the purchase price to be in tangible assets, to include whatever machinery and equipment, furniture and fixtures, inventory, and working capital are required to run the company.

If the seller wants to strip away the current assets, then the buyer needs to provide money for the purchase of the company plus working capital.

Where the growth has been over 15% annually, expect either a higher EBIT multiple or to negotiate an earn-out.

To summarize, about five times EBIT is the value of a debt-free company. If there is debt and the buyer is to assume it, then that amount is deducted. For example:

If EBIT is $800,000 times multiple of 5, the value of the company is:	$4,000,000
If the buyer is to assume the interest-bearing debt of:	700,000
The net proceeds to the seller would be:	$3,300,000

Since the repeal of the General Utilities Doctrine under the Tax Reform Act of 1986, many corporate sellers are subject to two separate taxes, one for the corporation and one for the individual. Thus the taxes due on capital gains on the sale of a business can reach as high as 50%.

When buyers prefer an asset sale, they must understand that the taxes to the seller will probably be higher than they would be on a stock sale; therefore, the seller will try to get more money for an asset sale.

How to Prepare an EBIT Worksheet for a Type B Company

In preparing an EBIT worksheet for the sale of a type B company, follow the same guidelines as for a type A company (see Exhibit 6-1).

Exhibits 6-5 and 6-6 show typical completed EBIT worksheets for type B companies. The company shown in Exhibit 6-5

(text continues on page 128)

Exhibit 6-5. Stock sale: type B company.

Re: File # _B209_ in $000s.

Fiscal year ending	2 yr. prior	1 yr. prior	Last year	Projection	
Sales	8,600	10,700	12,000		
Pretax from P&L	740	1,807	2,006		
Normalizing adjustments					
1. Interest paid	140	150	160		
2.					
3. Owner's benefits &					
4. salaries, perks	425	512	644		
5.					
6. Inventory valuation	155	290	250		
7.					
8. 2 managers' salaries	(331)	(360)	(383)		
9.					
10.					
11. EBIT normalized	1,129	2,149	2,677		
12. EBIT as % of sales	13%	20%	22%		%
13. + Depreciation	176	216	240		
14. = Cash flow (EBDIT)	1,305	2,363	2,917		

Comments: Outstanding management, dept. heads strong in Purchasing, Production, Personnel, Sales, Plant Manager—good consistent earnings, good back-up.

$2,677,000
× 5
$13,385,000   for 100% debt-free company

From Balance Sheet

Date: _____

Net Book Value (Omit all intangibles, like goodwill)	$2,830
Add Adjustments: Inventory reserve	2,500
Real Estate:	
Appraisal	_____
Less:	
book value	_____
	_____
Other Fixed Assets:	
Appraisal	2,700
Less:	
book value	900
	1,600
Other assets previously depreciated or expensed*	
*(list on reverse side)	330
Normalized	$7,260
Net Book Value Without Intangibles	

From Balance Sheet
Working Capital $1,550

Current Portion of
Long-Term Debt $ 177

Long-Term Debt $1,300

Tangible net worth   =   7,260   = 54%
Value of debt-free co.   13.385

Exhibit 6-6. Stock sale: type B company (very well managed, strong people in marketing and production).

Re: File # B702 in $000s.

Fiscal year ending	2 yr. prior	1 yr. prior	Last year	Projection
Sales	7,425	8,427	9,322	
Pretax from P&L	498	537	632	
Normalizing adjustments				
1. Interest paid	92	97	141	
2. Owner's salary & perks	335	361	391	
3. Owner's pension	37	42	47	
4.				
5. Rent to market price	(95)	(95)	(95)	
6.				
7. New manager's salary	(100)	(110)	(120)	
8.				
9.				
10.				
11. EBIT normalized	767	832	996	
12. EBIT as % of sales	10.3%	9.8%	10.6%	%
13. + Depreciation	151	166	186	
14. = Cash flow (EBDIT)				

From Balance Sheet

Date: _____

Net Book Value
(Omit all intangibles,
like goodwill) $1,950

Add Adjustments:
  Inventory reserve   300

Real Estate:
  Appraisal   _____
Less:
  book value   _____

Other Fixed Assets:
  Appraisal   2,725
Less:
  book value   1,720   1,005

Other assets previously
depreciated or expensed*
*(list on reverse side)

Normalized $3,255
Net Book Value Without Intangibles

From Balance Sheet

Working Capital $2,300

Current Portion of
Long-Term Debt $ 740

Long-Term Debt $ 850

Comments: Type B.
Reasonable price $996,000 × 5 = $4,980,000
for a debt-free company   = $5,000,000

Tangible net worth = $3.255 / $5MM = 65% of price will be tangible net worth
Value of debt-free company

Real estate owned by owner and family—adjust rent to market price.

has outstanding management that plans to remain after the sale, with good back-up in place. Earnings have been strong and consistent. A reasonable price for this company would be about $13.4 million, which is five times last year's EBIT.

Similarly, a reasonable price for the company in Exhibit 6.6 would be about $5 million, which is five times last year's EBIT of $996,000.

Some Additional Rules About EBIT Pricing

1. There is an exception to every rule.
2. Prices are a product of the current market.
3. Multiples vary with the size of the deal: The bigger the deal, within ranges, the higher the multiple.

Here are some very general guidelines on current multiples in the market:

1. For companies with sales up to about $20 million, the multiple is between $4^1/_2$ and $5^1/_2$.
2. For companies with sales from about $20 million to $75 million, the multiple ranges from $5^1/_2$ to $6^1/_2$.
3. For companies with sales from about $75 million to $125 million, the multiple hovers around 7.

Investment bankers tell me that there is a limit. If someone pays over an 8 multiple on a large deal, chances are he would be unable to pay off the debt on a leveraged sale.

To get multiples in these ranges, the seller needs good luck and sharp negotiating skills. He must also hope that the forces of supply and demand are aligned for his benefit.

In order for the buyer to pay multiples in the upper ranges, he must expect that:

1. The seller has had consistent growth, above average and without interruption, for the last three, four, or five years.
2. The seller has strong and experienced management in place.
3. There will be some beneficial characteristics, such as a

special niche, special customers, or superior marketing and service techniques.

4. The seller's competitive advantage will not erode, or a calamity will not occur (as in a case where the seller had been relying on one giant customer and the customer disappeared).

7
About Negotiation

Two partners in the clothing business decided to diversify, and one of the partners was delegated to go to Florida to look for an investment. A week later partner 1 called partner 2.

Partner 1:   I think we can make a deal. We can buy the Ritz Hotel for only $40 million.

Partner 2:   That's great!

Partner 1:   But there's a catch.

Partner 2:   What's the catch?

Partner 1:   They want $5,000 down.

I expect both parties to stake out maximum positions before the negotiations—but both parties are flexible and might change their positions as the talks progress.
            —*Former Secretary of State Cyrus Vance*

Two old friends meet. ''Sam,'' says one, ''Have I got a deal for you. I can let you have a full-grown hippopotamus for $100.''

    ''Are you kidding?'' says Sam. ''My wife and kids live in a three-room apartment. What am I going to do with a hippopotamus?''

    ''Okay, okay,'' says the first man. ''You drive a tough bargain. How about two for $150?''

    Sam nodded. ''You got yourself a deal.''

Some Random Thoughts About Negotiating

B UYERS tend to fall into three categories:

1. Those who bargain for everything.
2. Those who decide that their first price is their last price. (In one very successful company, the principal hates to bargain. He knows what he wants from the seller, and how much he is willing to pay for it.)
3. Those very much like #2 but who are willing to compromise.

One buyer comes in a little on the low side for openers saying that there is no sense putting everything on the table, that he must leave room to pay a higher price in the future. If someone wants to pay what he considers to be an above-market price, he deserves to get it.

One seller feels that no one will pay the first price, so he starts a little high. He says he had heard that there should be a negotiating cushion of 5–15%.

One professional intermediary says he likes to go in on the high side, to expose the company to a large group of qualified buyers, and hope that there will emerge a special buyer who sees things the same way he does and who will pay a top price.

In a recent situation that was shown to nine prospects, five felt that the company was overpriced, two felt the price was slightly high, and two thought it was a fair price. One of the latter bought the company. The first group were asset buyers, who would not pay a premium over the adjusted book value.

As one buyer said recently:

I have been through the agony and frustration and experience of losing a good opportunity and at the last minute being outbid. I will say now what I would not have said three months ago: I am willing to pay the premium."

Obviously, if you have a bitter taste in your mouth from having lost the last few deals, you might now want a deal so badly that you will probably pay more.

Price negotiation may be based on last year's actual EBIT, or this year's projection, if it is firm. If the seller asks for a little more than he expects and then compromises, both the buyer and seller feel good because they both win.

A decision must be made by the seller whether the company is to be shown to one buyer in a particular time frame, or if it is to be shown to more than one buyer at a time.

Nick Wellner, a master deal maker, says he once closed a $28 million deal in 45 days, start to finish. He says he was able to do it (1) because he has a good deal-making lawyer and (2) because he does not have to ask too many people too many questions.

Other experts feel that the principals should do the negotiating in the early stages without the presence of lawyers and accountants. Of course, the seller should be checking with the advisers about the negotiation but should not get sidetracked early on. One good piece of advice is never to commit yourself to a material point unless everything is on the table. If it is a substantial issue, you should know what else is to be discussed and settled.

Negotiation Means Compromise

A friend was trying to buy a company and was being stalled. The owner just would not make a decision. There were delays and delays, and finally the buyer said, "Look, I can't go on any longer, I have other things to do. I need to know in one week." He walked away. A few weeks later, the sale of the company was announced. Apparently, the owner had been negotiating with other prospects.

In another situation, the seller owned a building financed by a state agency at subsidized rates. Part of the agreement with the state provided that in the event the company was sold, the rental on the building could not be raised. The seller decided to rent the building to the buyer at a below-market price, and the seller was able to make up the difference with an extra component in his advisory service agreement.

You cannot discuss pricing a company in a vacuum. The horse trade is between people, and so prospective buyers and sellers are going to be involved in the human side of the deal. That usually means compromise. A wise man said: "Nobody gets everything he wants."

The following section should provide some insight about what might be coming up in negotiations besides money issues.

Objectives of Buyers and Sellers

The following is one of the best sets of written objectives I have seen to cover the conflicting views and needs of buyer and seller. It appeared in a Small Business Administration publication entitled *Buying and Selling a Small Business*, by Verne A. Bunn.

> The final objective of the negotiation process is a written agreement covering the details of the proposed buy-sell transaction. Some of the details—price, terms of payment, price allocation, form of the transaction, liabilities, warranties—are matters over which the interests and motivations of the buyer and seller may be in sharp conflict.
>
> The seller is interested in:
>
> - The best possible price
> - Getting his or her money
> - Favorable tax treatment of gains from the sale
> - Severing liability ties, past and future
> - Avoiding contract terms and conditions that he or she may not be able to carry out
>
> In contrast, the buyer is interested in:
>
> - A good title at the lowest possible price.
> - Favorable payment terms.
> - A favorable tax basis for resale and depreciation purposes.
> - Warranty protection against false statements of the seller,

inaccurate financial data, and undisclosed or potential liabilities.

· An indemnification agreement and security deposit. The agreement reached by the parties—if they succeed in reaching one—will be the result of bargaining. Depending on the relative bargaining position of the buyer and seller, the buy-sell contract may reflect either compromise or capitulation.

Strategic Approaches

The seller's primary mission is not to sell the business. The primary mission is to get paid for the business. The mission is to sell the company at a satisfactory price, and to make sure that payment is received when it is wanted, and in the way it is wanted.

Negotiations for settling the price terms of a deal run the gamut of behaviors that I can illustrate with two people I will call client 1 and client 2.

Client 1 is a rich, successful entrepreneur who does not enjoy the give-and-take of horse trading. He has bought several sizable companies. He is very astute and does his homework. He tells the seller, "Your company would be worth X dollars to us." If he can't buy it at that price, he walks away. He says "I know pretty much how much I'm willing to pay, and that's what I offer. I don't have time to waste."

Client 2 is also rich and successful. But I think he got his training from a Levantine rug merchant. To do business with him almost rips your heart from your body. Dealing with him means you bargain, haggle, chaffer, wrangle, higgle, propose, counterpropose. Finally, you compromise to make the deal. Not everyone can deal with this person, for whom bargaining is a way of life. You need to be patient, good-natured, and very interested.

It is not uncommon for the seller to give a price, and for the buyer to reject the price and walk away with this happening

10 times before the serious bargaining begins. The seller does not get insulted if, for example, she asks a price of 100, and the buyer counters with an offer of 15. "Impossible," says the seller. "But I will sell it for 80." "No," says the buyer, "it's only worth 20." Back and forth, back and forth, until finally the deal is struck between 30 and 50, depending on the interest of the buyer and the negotiating skills of both the buyer and the seller. In many places, the seller would be insulted if you paid what was asked and would look upon you as a fool.

Sometimes the counteroffer is refused and the seller walks away without trying to drag you back. So if the ploy of bargaining doesn't work, change the method. You have nothing to lose by trying.

When buying, don't appear to be in a hurry, or too anxious; you will not get your price. It seems to hold true that if you don't ask, you don't get. What have you got to lose by trying? The worst that will happen if you cannot get a cut in price is that you will have to pay the full asking price. It is best always to ask.

Then there is the buyer who learned his bargaining techniques at the "flea market." (Frankly, the technique often works, especially if the seller is in a hurry to sell and/or there are no other buyers.) This buyer feels it is a sin to pay the asking price. For openers, he starts at about one-half the desired price and keeps going up (if he has to)—unless he finds flaws, in which case he'll bargain for a lower price.

Most people think that they are experts in bargaining. When was the last time *you* paid sticker price for a car?

Some of the conversations in the sale of a business might run like the following—even if the selling price is stated in the presentation package.

> "What's your asking price?" (Asking price denotes a starting point.) I've heard a skillful seller say something like, "Our price is not an asking price. We have set a price range of between [for example, $3–3.25 million], depending on what kind of deal we do."

> The skillful buyer might ask, "What are your terms, and asking price?" (He's really putting the seller on the defensive.) The prospect is thinking about terms and again talks about the asking price.

Sometimes someone wants to buy a company that has not been offered for sale. As a matter of fact, the owner has not even thought of selling the company. Later when they meet to discuss a possible sale, the buyer will try every which way to get the seller to put a price on the company. Who knows what the seller will say? The buyer can always counter with a lower price. The seller, if alert, will persist and not give a price but might counter with "*You* came looking for *me*. How much will you offer?" In desperation the buyer says, "But the seller always has the offering price. I won't put a price on your company."

Oh, how delicious it is to watch this kind of bargaining. Everything depends on who is worn out first—and how anxious the buyer is to buy and how anxiously the seller wants to sell.

Negotiating is the way to horse trade. By giving and taking, it cannot all go one way or for the benefit of one party. The bargaining starts to come together, and then there are compromises among the various trade-offs and alternatives, and lo! the deal is done. In the end, both will have been satisfied or else there will be no deal.

Factors in the Negotiated Price

Not too many deals are closed on a take-it-or-leave-it basis. The price and deal depend on a number of things. You can almost always bet and win that the company will not be sold for fair market value. What determines the price? The negotiated price depends on:

1. The tax situation of the buyer and the seller.
2. Supply and demand. How badly does the seller need or want to sell? How badly does the buyer need or want to buy?
3. The horse-trading abilities of the buyer and the seller. Who is negotiating for the buyer and the seller? Is one side afraid of losing the deal?
4. Good luck (finding the right customer at the right time), or what is known as a "caprice of fortune."
5. The economy: Are you selling at a time when the busi-

ness outlook is optimistic or pessimistic? Is money tight or loose?

6. Whether the buyer can afford the deal.

Horse Sense About the Negotiating Process

Here are a few additional thoughts about the negotiating process leading to a successful horse trade:

1. Make no misleading statements.
2. Be surprised and amazed if you close on the scheduled closing date. Things do have a way of getting delayed or fouled up. So leave yourself a little leeway.
3. Tie most of your plans and proposals together with an elastic band, not a steel strap. Beware the deadlock. Give your negotiator a way to save face in a final, absolute-offer situation.

In an attempt to get a concession, buyers will argue that they will not be able to retain all the old customers.

Or that they will have to spend a lot of extra money on travel and entertainment (T&E) to get to know the customers, so earnings will suffer while they are spending money to cultivate the customers.

Or that it will take a long period to learn the business and the company.

Or, if the earnings go down, that they will not be able to service the debt with a reduced cash flow.

The seller will argue that there was plenty of opportunity to expand but he or she did not want to. Let the new owner expand; the company is a gold mine.

Or, that he's been paying lots of personal expenses through the company and has been holding down the earnings.

Or the buyer will be increasing his equity as he continues to make his debt-service payments.

And so on, forth and back, back and forth, until there is a deal.

> *Keep the mission in mind. The seller's mission is to get paid for the company she or he is selling. Negotiate toward that end.*

How Is the Deal to Be Structured?

1. Is it a sale for assets?
2. Is it a sale for stock?
3. Is everything to be sold?
4. What is being retained by the owner? What is to be leased, and what are the terms?
5. How is the sales price to be allocated? What are the tax consequences to the buyer and to the seller? (There are conflicting interests of the buyer and the seller. Some items will be deductible to the buyer, some items will give ordinary income to the seller, and some will give capital gains.)

How Is the Deal to Be Paid For?

1. Stock
2. All cash
3. Part cash, and part something else
4. What is the security and collateral?
5. What is the interest rate?
6. How is the price to be cut up:
   • Sale price?
   • Contingencies?
   • Noncompete agreement?
   • Employment contract?
   • Consultant fees?
   • Royalties?
   • Leases?
   • Down payment?
   • Installment sale?
   • Private annuity?

Contingency payouts (so much now, more later) are usually based on sales or earnings. However, they can also use other measures, such as retained customers, cash flow, return on operating assets, or whatever the two decide and agree on. It can be a fixed amount or a multiple. It can be level payments, with a big balloon payment at the end. The interest rates can be adjusted up or down to help offset and control the ordinary income or the capital gains.

The seller may decide that he wants to sell just the operating assets and retain the real estate, the equipment, or other fixed assets and lease them back to the buyer. That method eliminates the recapture problem of depreciation and investment tax credits and defers the capital-gains problem. In some cases the seller may also retain patents and will continue to collect royalties or license fees.

If the buyer is a public company and the seller decides to accept stock, the seller may be able to get a guarantee or falling price protection, in case the stock price is down when you are ready to sell.

There are problems with letter stock, so make sure you understand the restrictions of when and how you can sell the stock. You might get common stock, voting preferred, or convertible debentures, maybe even warrants. If you collect interest instead of dividends, the instrument you received is probably a debt.

How to Ensure Payment if the Deal Is Not All Cash

Here is some advice about security for the seller.

Talk is cheap. Remember, your mission is to get paid for the business you sell.

If you do not get cash for the business you sell, then some of the methods of securing money that is owed to you—even if you have an installment sale—include getting:

1. A pledge of assets or stock.
2. A first mortgage.
3. Personal guarantees from the buyer or a third party (for

example, a relative, if the buyer is not strong enough). The money you protect is your own.
4. Security agreements.
5. Conditional sales contracts.

Generally, the higher the risk of getting paid, the higher the price. The stronger the security and/or the deposit, the lower the price.

Some of the best advice ever given on negotiating was that of James E. Robinson. This is a segment of a speech he gave to the Association for Corporate Growth.*

"Now then, if, however, it still breaks down, I have one last piece of advice to offer you which I think in my experience has been very, very valuable. This has to do with advice which was given to me years ago when I was a young man. An older man was counseling me in a particular situation in which I felt I was being outrageously mistreated. I was ready to throw the whole thing over and tell all the other guys to go to hell. And I'll never forget what this man said to me. "Jim," he said, "as you go through this vale of tears called life, you will in fact miss many, many opportunities. There will be things that come up that you do not see and later you will kick yourself in the pants because you didn't seize that opportunity when it presented itself. But there is one opportunity which you will never miss, and that is the opportunity to tell them to go to hell. The first time it comes up, you don't have to do it. You can always do it the next day, the next week—or a year later—maybe never."

And that has really stood me in good stead. I have been in situations where I felt the other guy was really being absolutely outrageously unreasonable, and had the almost uncontrollable urge to tell him to go to hell. But I contained that urge, just put the deal aside and put it back in the file—and hoped that it might come

*J. E. Robinson, in *Intergrowth '78: The Evolving Pattern of Corporate Growth* (Glenview, IL: Association for Corporate Growth, 1978). Reprinted with permission.

alive another date—and that has actually happened to me. So no matter how frustrated you may be or how unreasonable you think the other guy is, if the deal does not go through, don't tell him to go to hell. You can always do that later.

Some Additional Advice From Deal Makers That May Help to Make the Deal

- One buyer likes to pick up small companies and likes to structure deals at book value with no allocation to goodwill, and put in all the extras into agreements and contracts that can be expensed or amortized.
- "What kind of price have you put on the company?" This is language taken from the art dealer's world. The question implies that the price is a starting point.
- "Nobody has to do anything that is not in the agreement. You might get something that is not in the agreement, if you pay a price for it—like cut the price."
- "Under the first amendment, you can't make a person stay on the job. You might sue them for a breach, but you can't make them stay."
- "When a prospect asks a question, sometimes you can ignore answering it—but if it's asked a second time, don't ignore it. It's important."
- One interesting negotiation involved a company that was for sale and losing money. The investor decided to lend the company money and took back a note plus a purchase option from the seller. That gave him the position of a creditor and an opportunity to buy the company if it were turned around.
- One interesting deal was closed recently where the seller agreed to a sale for book value and half the earnings for the next four years.
- Sometimes a deal is put together, and then the buyer discovers that he cannot arrange the financing. Sometimes the seller, in order to save the deal, will renegotiate at a higher price and handle the financing himself.
- Sometimes a seller doesn't have a broker, and if he is a

nervous type or cannot deal with negotiations because of the frustrations and arguments incidental to a negotiation, he will hire someone to negotiate for him.

- A salesperson must know when to be quiet so that the prospect can have time to sell herself on the deal, without any interruption. I have seen good sellers ask the question and remain silent for 10 minutes while the buyer was mulling it over in her mind. Saying anything would have interrupted her train of thought.

- I know buyers who think that if the profits are tied to a seller who is to continue to work with a company, the buyer will pay for the tangible assets up front and tie the premium portion of future contingency payments based on performance.

- Selling a business is like selling an antique to a dealer. Know what you have for sale and how much you want for it. If you do not know what it is worth, find out before you start showing it to the dealers. Do your homework. Then you must find out who the best prospect is.

- You can negotiate for anything you want: health plan, car, club benefits. I know one man who wanted secretarial service from the company for two years after he left.

- Proprietary process, a proprietary product, and/or a sophisticated technology, can be transferred.

- Generally, whether a deal is to be for cash or other than cash depends on the tax situation of the seller and the money situation of the buyer.

- If you sell the company on credit (for example, an installment sale) you can usually get a higher price. Generally, the more the credit and the greater the risk, the higher the price. To repeat the old saying, "It's not how much, but how. Let me structure the deal and I'll pay you almost any price."

- One creative seller had stayed on after the sale as the new president. He had sold the company with an earn-out clause. One of the accounts receivable was beginning to sour, and it appeared that it might become a $10,000 bad debt. The seller/manager determined he was better off to pay the customer's account out of his pocket at a cost of $10,000. The trade-off, of course, was that by paying

$10,000 out of pocket, the earnings were not reduced—and on those earnings of $10,000 he earned a multiple of 5. The net result was that he earned an extra $50,000 at a cost of $10,000, with a net benefit of $40,000.

- Normally, an intermediary will not hold a proposal exclusively for a prospect unless she has a strong response or a very serious intent from a prospect, and then she will want some understanding about how long the exclusive will remain an exclusive. Deals do have a way of stretching out and cooling off, and an intermediary's job is to keep things moving along.

Where to Negotiate

Here are some suggestions about the atmosphere of the negotiation, about where to meet with a seller who wants to arrange a meeting with a broker or a buyer.

If the seller does not care if anyone knows that his company is for sale, or if the employees know that the boss is trying to sell the company, then there is no harm in the intermediary's going to the seller's office. However, if confidentiality and secrecy are necessary, then there are a few things to think about.

The initial meeting, either between seller and intermediary's or buyer and seller, should not be held in the owner's office, or at a restaurant. Someone may recognize the broker and put two and two together. "I saw So-and-So with Mr. Intermediary. So-and-So must have his company up for sale." Also, third parties can overhear you or interrupt you. Think about meeting in the intermediary's office, or the owner's home, or the attorney or accountant's office. One intermediary almost always arranges the first meeting at a motel about 30 miles from the seller's location.

Secrecy is imperative to avoid the problems that might develop prematurely with employees and competitors.

Another point: Some buyers and sellers like to take phone calls about a pending deal only at home, not at the company office. It is easy enough for both parties to agree on a mutually convenient time to call.

Some sellers do not have any of the confidential mail sent to the company. Instead, it is sent to the home or to the attorney's office.

Employees are especially smart and seem to have an intelligence network that the CIA would envy. This is particularly true in small towns, where everyone knows everyone. Once suspicions are aroused, rumors will multiply. If care is not taken, the employees will start getting their resumes out.

Attitudes and Personalities

While you are in the negotiating process, try to remember the following:

> You are dealing with a person's feelings, and you must convince the person that he or she is being treated fairly.
> There may be honest differences of opinion about value.
> Are both parties listening?
> It takes time to negotiate.
> Do not be "too busy."
> Do not expect everything to be logical. Many decisions are based on attitudes and feelings.

Timing must be convenient for both parties. When you start getting into the nitty-gritty, see if you and the buyer can agree on what you will talk about at the next meeting. Or work with an agenda so you know what has to be covered at the next meeting. It helps cut down the drag-out time.

In dealing with a larger company, after the opening meeting with the principal, it is useful to ask, "Will you be the person I'll be working with from now on?" The answer will be a "Yes," or "No," or "See Ms. So-and-So from now on."

Everyone is unique, with different desires, attitudes, and personality. So each negotiation is going to be different. One seller applies what he learned in a course from the Mitchell Institute, which teaches selling methods. Their technique is based on a theory that people who look alike buy alike, and all want to be treated the same way. According to their teachings, if you have certain physical characteristics, you will be motivated by the same things that others with your characteristics have.

Another seller never makes a presentation to a prospective buyer early on in the process if that buyer is a pipe smoker. He feels that pipe smokers are thinkers, not activists. He saves the pipe-smoking prospects for later. They never get first crack at a deal. Another seller told me that he used to work in the south many years ago in a retail store, and he hated to wait on nut eaters (whether peanuts, Indian nuts, or pistachios). Nut eaters were very slow to make a decision.

Two successful sellers I know have yet other criteria. One makes selling appointments according to the prospect's bio-rhythm chart (when he can get the prospect's birth date). If he or the prospect is having a double-critical (or a triple-critical) day, he won't make an appointment for that day. The other person uses a book called *Astrology for Lovers* to see how he can expect to get along with his prospect astrologically.

Here are some thoughts on what can affect negotiations positively or negatively:

1. *Authority*. Try not to get bogged down with people who do not have the authority to make a decision.
2. *Pricing*. Price is affected by the economic outlook. Is the business outlook optimistic, or pessimistic? Is financing easy to get, or tight? If difficult, the seller may have to go down in price to make the sale. If the financing is tight, the seller may be willing to finance, and the value of the credit is worth a premium.
3. *Supply and demand*. What is the supply and demand situation for that kind of company at the moment? Are there too many sellers and not enough buyers? Has some new technology come into the market that will make the company's machinery obsolete, or will some new competition arise from the blue?
4. *Seller's mood*. What is the seller's mood? Is she too anxious? Is she afraid of losing or making a deal, so that she is mentally set to do a deal at any price? Maybe she has already started to picture herself sitting under the palm trees and wants to get rid of the company in a hurry. This state lowers her bargaining powers.
5. *Earnings*. Obviously, the best time to get the "best" price is when your earnings are terrific. Are your earnings terrific?
6. *Timing*. Can you imagine why a 75-year-old-man probably would not be keen about a 20-year payout to a stranger?

7. *Expectations.* A recent deal fell through after a buyer and seller had agreed on 10 times earnings. The buyer expected to pay 10 times the after-tax earnings. The seller expected 10 times the pretax earnings, which is almost a 20-year payback. The deal fell through. Never take anything for granted. Say it aloud, and make sure you know whether you are talking about pretax or after-tax.

8. *Keep cool.* Remember that negotiating is a horse trade. If you are fair, and if you do things right, you will end up with the horse. If you lose your cool, you will probably lose the deal. Good horse traders do not lose their cool.

Master Checklist for Sellers

The following is a good checklist of items that the seller should have information about.

☐ Are there any unrecorded obligations—like contingencies for pending lawsuits?

☐ Does the seller have the right to transfer leases or contracts?

☐ Will the seller's personal guarantees on contracts be released? Will the lessor accept the new buyer?

☐ What is the value of previously expensed items still in use, such as R&D, the value of special tools, and drawings?

☐ What is the value of fully depreciated assets still in use?

☐ What is the special value of the company name, image, logos, or proprietary names?

☐ What kind of regulatory agency violations are pending?

☐ The buyer might be interested in the seller's staff, or in any special technology and know-how, the customer lists, customer locations, or patents.

☐ What are the contingent liabilities?

☐ What is the reputation of the company with customers?

☐ How do you value work-in-process? Patents and copyrights?

☐ The buyer will want to examine federal and state tax returns, insurance policies, corporation papers, and stock registers. There have been too many suits against certified public accounting firms. So even if you have a good, clean opinion letter attached to the financials, do not be surprised if the prospective buyer requests his own audit. In the closing statement do not be surprised if the buyer expects an indemnification clause regarding possible assessment of additional federal taxes for the unaudited years.

I know a company that has no product liability insurance. They say they cannot afford it, and if it were made mandatory they would have to close down the company. They do not feel threatened because they have no consumer customers. On that note, how would a buyer reserve for a potential exposure under the Consumer Products Safety Code? How would the IRS treat the reserves—maybe as a retention of funds?

- [ ] What nonroutine purchase orders are pending?
- [ ] Is there a list of credits being held by other companies for the seller?
- [ ] Are there some reserve and allowance accounts being held for the seller?
- [ ] What is the patent protection?
- [ ] Which activities are profitable?
- [ ] Which activities are not profitable?
- [ ] As the prospect walks around the plant, store, or office, the seller should list the assets that are not part of the sale.
- [ ] What articles in use are leased?
- [ ] What items are on consignment and belong to customer? Dies? Jigs?
- [ ] The buyer will expect to examine executive compensation agreements.
- [ ] The buyer will expect to see a list of all depreciable assets.
- [ ] The buyer will expect to see licensing agreements.
- [ ] The buyer will want to know about the customers, their type, and the number.
- [ ] The buyer will want to know about the vendors.

Attention, sellers: Buyers will probably want to talk about items that are off the balance sheet and that might have an effect on earnings, so be prepared to talk about them. As examples, in the area of contingent liabilities these might include:

- [ ] Repurchase agreements
- [ ] Past service liabilities, regarding pension plan and the like
- [ ] Pending lawsuits
- [ ] Deferred bonus arrangements
- [ ] Profit-sharing plans

- [ ] Was there a write down of inventory in the last three years?
- [ ] Financial leases
- [ ] Covenant-not-to-compete contract
- [ ] Union contracts
- [ ] Sales or loan contracts that might have negatives
- [ ] What debts are due, and when? Will there be enough money to make the payments?
- [ ] Uncompleted contracts
- [ ] Unbilled services
- [ ] Customer accounts sold with recourse
- [ ] Security agreements
- [ ] Assets pledged
- [ ] Is the company the guarantor for others on notes on contracts?
- [ ] Are any bonds open regarding unfinished contracts?
- [ ] What purchase commitments are outstanding?
- [ ] Environmental and OSHA issues
- [ ] What are the amounts of deposits or advances from customers' leases, if any?
- [ ] Vacations or other benefits owing to employees for current year
- [ ] Any product liability
- [ ] Any deferred charges the company is involved in

Any of the above could affect the kind of deal the buyer is willing to become involved in. If there is any of risk of possible exposure, he or she may not want to make the deal.

On the other hand, if there is good news that is off the balance sheet, make sure you prepare a schedule for that too. In some businesses there are annual settlements of credits, and allowances and reserves. Make sure that you include that amount in your list of values that you want to get paid for.

The seller (or his agent) must be both thinker and salesperson. He must think of all the things that will make the seller's company look good or better, such as what expenses the new purchaser will not have. For example, who is retiring next year and the year after and probably will not be replaced? Remember that for every dollar you can save for the prospective buyer, you might get five dollars extra for your business.

Special Advice for the Buyer

Here are a few suggestions for the buyer:

1. If you discover that the seller is less than honest, stop the deal. In the long run you will be happier.

2. Be a salesman. Don't be a ruffian. You are on a selling mission, trying to buy on the terms most favorable for you or for your company. Your mission is to convince and argue and horse trade, not to brow-beat, or impugn, or derogate. A good salesman is a lover.

3. Do not be afraid to ask sensitive questions, but do so with tact. If things are bothering you, you might as well ask the questions up front and clear the air. The questions you hate to ask have to be faced sooner or later. If you are an entrepreneurial type, you are intelligent and assertive enough to figure out how to ask, or get your intermediary to inquire on your behalf.

4. There really is not a buyer's market or a seller's market. There is a market for good, profitable companies. If you find one, coddle it. There are probably 60 buyers for each good company. Most companies you consider have some kind of problem.

5. Make sure that the lawyer to whom you look for advice or to handle the closing is experienced in such commercial transactions as the purchase or sale of a business. If you do not think your lawyer has the experience, hire a lawyer for this special purchase or sale only. You should not have a lawyer represent you who is not in familiar territory.

6. If you want the owner-manager to continue working, tell her how you would like to integrate her into your plan and what you would expect. There is no point in springing surprises, or having her disgruntled, or having her quit because of misunderstandings that could have been avoided. If you have other companies that are being run by happy ex-owner-managers, have the prospective seller meet them to find out what a great guy and boss you are.

7. Comfort the seller about your deep sense of trustworthiness, and that you'll keep the talk about the sale of the business confidential. Generally, the seller does not want employees or competitors to hear that the company is for sale before the sale is made. It creates too many problems.

8. Do not play the big shot or act overconfident and arrogant. Do not say, "I'm a professional manager; I can run any business," because that kind of immodesty can cause much heartache. Every business has its own peculiarities, so there are caveats about tackling a new company in a new locale

or in a new field. There is nothing wrong with being a little modest!

9. Do not forget to do your homework to make sure that the numbers work out, and that you are aware of any significant changes going on in the industry. What good is the purchase if it does not have adequate earnings and cash flow? Double check with your financial adviser and develop a pro forma cash flow. Make sure that you are not overpaying for the business.

10. Finally, if you as the seller are dealing with a large company, it may be that the person you are dealing with is the negotiator, and not the decision-maker. One very large corporation sends out a two-person team to work out a deal. One is the negotiator, who must have each and every agreement approved by the decision-maker, who is not in the same room as the negotiator. It is their way of doing deals, and if you want to do business with them, that is how it is done.

8

Why Companies
Do Not Sell
and
Why Some Deals
Fall Apart

How awful, how devastating to have a deal collapse, after there has been a public announcement.

The bottom can fall out when the seller depends on one buyer.

If you can't finance it, you can't sell it.
                                        —*A broker*

The Anatomy of a Deal and Its Possible Collapse

I N the normal sequence of events:

1. The seller finally finds a buyer.
2. The parties come to terms, agree on a deal, and sign a letter of intent.
3. After the letter of intent comes the due diligence.
4. After the due diligence comes the preparation of the purchase and sales agreement.
5. Finally comes the closing, and the company is transferred.

It is important for the seller to remember that a buyer can sign a letter of intent and still walk away from the deal—generally a letter of intent is not binding on the buyer. It does, however, require the seller to take her company off the market for a set period of time. Normally, the letter of intent gives the terms and conditions of the proposed sale and details about whether the transaction will be a stock or asset deal; how much, and/or how the price is to be determined; how the payment is to be made; expected agreements covering noncompete conditions and employment; special issues regarding real estate, confidentiality, and agreement to remove the company from sale to other parties; the proposed signing date of the purchase and sales agreement; and the closing date.

When the parties to the transaction are both private (not public) companies, there is no compulsion to make a public disclosure. A public disclosure announces to the important people (the employees, the creditors, the customers, and the competitors) that there is a possible sale pending. And *what a disaster it is then if the deal does not go to completion.* Most sellers would like to keep the negotiations of the pending sale secret. One seller went through three letters of intent only to have the deal collapse. Imagine what impact it had on him psychologically and emotionally. The company was finally sold on the fourth try, and he collected his money. But what a difficult, anxious seller he was up to the closing.

After the signing of the letter of intent comes the due diligence by the lawyer and the accountants. During this process, the buyer's representatives try to make sure that all the representations are true, and to uncover any unstated problems that would affect the future. It is during this period that the buyer must make sure that nothing is taken for granted. In addition to confirming all balance-sheet items, the buyer needs to learn about any possible environmental problems, any pending lawsuits, or any recent changes in the industry. The buyer also must make sure that there will not be an exodus of the people who made the numbers possible.

Next comes the preparation of the *purchase and sales agreement,* the binding agreement. This contract, which can run 75– 100 pages, lists the terms and conditions of the sale, and the responsibilities and obligations of the buyer and the seller. It states the seller's warranties, guarantees, and indemnifications. This part of the process is the most dangerous, because it presents the greatest opportunity for deals to fall apart. Normally the client whose lawyer prepares the documents has the advantage. The lawyer preparing the documents may take certain liberties, leaving the other party open to discovering issues or changes that had never been agreed to.

There is also a problem area that exists when the two law firms are not peers, that is, when one of the firms is a big, deal-making firm and the other party is represented by a lawyer inexperienced in making deals. Lawyers for big firms also tend to be under terrific time pressure. Although they may have three weeks to prepare the agreements, somehow many do not get started until a few days before the proposed signing date. Often the lawyer for the other party, who is under great pressure to examine the documents, starts to discover clauses that her party never agreed to. So the principals have to start negotiating again, and everyone gets hot and tense. But this time both sides have spent a lot of money for lawyers, accountants, and commitment letters.

Once all terms have been finally agreed to, there is the signing of the contracts. The deal is done when the contract is "signed, sealed, and delivered."

Deal Killers

Among the greatest sources of stress and distress to both a buyer and a seller are the "deal killers": the things that can abort a deal, some of which may be beyond the control of either party. Others may be predictable, given the personalities that will be involved in the deal or transaction: the principals, the lawyers, the accountants, the bankers, the lenders. Experienced intermediaries learn never to spend their fees until they have collected them. Too many things can go wrong.

Consider a situation where everyone is in the lawyer's office for the closing (or the signing of the purchase and sales agreement), and at the last minute the seller starts to cry and says, "I can't do it, I can't go through with it, I thought I could, but I just can't sell the business! What will I do?" and walks out of the lawyer's office.

Or the "perfect deal" that was developing, when the buyer learns that a substantial part of the sales came from government contracts. The perfect buyer withdraws because he does not want to do business with the government. He once had a sorrowful experience and has vowed he will never work on another order for the government.

Or how about the situation where the seller assumed he could get a release as a personal guarantor on a lease and then discovers that the landlord is willing to transfer the lease to the new buyer but is unwilling to release the guarantor? The landlord is probably not obligated to release the original guarantor. Of course, the seller does not want the liability continuing into the future, or to be responsible after he sells the company. (Sometimes you can make a cash settlement with the landlord to get a release.)

Or you as the seller assume that the provider of the long-term loan (whether a bank, an insurance company, a venture capital company, or an SBIC) would be willing to accept the proposed new buyer in your place, and then discover that they are not willing. In some cases the agreement with the lender prohibits you from selling your company. Or you may have a prepayment penalty clause, or the lender will accept the new purchaser but only at a much higher interest rate. This can create a big problem when the purchaser has been developing the cash-flow projections assuming a 7% interest rate but now learns that the new rates will be higher. The previously calculated ROI is no longer pertinent.

Or the buyer might have run a security check, credit check, or character report with a company such as Fidelifacts, Bishop's, Hooper's, Pinkerton's, or Dun & Bradstreet. Perhaps the buyer will not like what is reported (and you will never know).

Or the professionals, the accountants and lawyers, do not deliver the work at the time they promised to deliver—they lack the sense of urgency that the principals expect, and the slowdown causes a cooling off. This may be the time for the principals to be assertive.

Or maybe you have a tactless lawyer, like the one who said at the closing, "I keep telling my client [the seller], he's selling the company too cheaply. I could have gotten him more." The deal was killed. The seller walked out. A new buyer was found seven months later and paid only 70% of the original buyer's deal. (One is reminded of the time Albert Einstein was interviewed and asked "What's the secret of success?" He answered, "There are three parts to success: Work hard, take time out to play, and know when to keep your mouth shut.")

Or—as hard as it may be to believe—your "perfect prospect" is negotiating on two other deals (unbeknownst to you). When she decides to close one of the other deals, she drops yours. She will thank you and tell you she has a full plate now.

Or you and the buyer cannot agree on the values of certain assets, or on who is to pay the broker's fees or legal fees, or the accounting fees.

Or the goodwill component in the deal is too much of a percentage of the deal. Sometimes a way must be found to reduce the goodwill component, since it can foul up the cash flow needed to do the deal. One deal was saved recently by working out an employment contract that provided a commission on sales to former customers over a three-year period, in lieu of part of the goodwill.

Or there was the situation where a lawyer fouled up a deal by recommending an installment sale with a contingency based on future earnings. The problem was that it would not be allowed to qualify as an installment sale unless the agreement mentioned a maximum price.

Or there is the misunderstanding about what a "net, net lease" is. One party's perception is that the maintenance is "from the street in," while the other party assumes that it is "from the walls in."

Or the lawyer for the seller prepared an agreement with about 50 conditions, all upon the buyer. The buyer almost walked out. The seller had to be told he could not have it all his way, that maybe the seller should have 25 conditions for the buyer, and that the buyer would have about 25 conditions for the seller. The seller had to be told that if he wanted to sell the company he had better start compromising or he would lose the prospect. The lawyer was trying to protect his client, but too much was too much.

Or a seller in a stock deal discovers that the securities that he was about to accept are nonvoting shares.

Or a sudden unexpected announcement of a competitive situation reduces the allure of the seller's company.

Or a key employee suddenly leaves or dies.

Or "things are not always what they seem. Skim milk masquerades as cream," such as the discovery of a skeleton in the closet, or that you have you been lied to or told half-truths.

Or the seller in a stock deal absolutely refuses to provide warranty, representation, and indemnification clauses.

Or the human breakdown, when people don't really listen, don't communicate, or don't trust each other.

Or maybe the buyer cannot handle the unfunded past service on the pension plan.

Or it is discovered that there are unexpected or unresolved environmental problems, or that an unexpected union action is about to begin, or that a lawsuit has been filed, or that nonmaintenance problems have developed, or that new legislation will affect the company.

Or how about the situation where the serious buyer says he wants an independent audit to be paid for by the seller? The seller says, "Okay, but first I want an agreement from you that you'll buy the company according to all the terms and conditions we've agreed upon. However, if then the audit turns up any misrepresentations or any negative disclosures not previously discussed, you can then be released from the agreement." An acquisition audit by an outside firm is not inexpensive. This forces the decision.

Or there is pressure on the seller to make additional concessions.

Or the buyer discovers that the seller has been paying bribes and kickbacks to get business. At a recent closing, just before the signing of the purchase and sales agreement, the seller asked the buyer how he felt about paying off a customer's representative to get business. The buyer walked away from the deal.

Or the seller demands more money because lots of new orders have just started to pour in, or she decides at the last minute to change the deal from a stock deal to an asset deal with significant tax consequences.

Or the financing, which the buyer thought he had, collapses. One buyer had investors who were going to back him in a purchase. Each investor told him, "Count me in." When the time came for the closing, not one of the five participated. They disappeared.

Or the seller does something dumb, like letting the buyer occupy an office and get involved with employees and customers before the closing.

Or there are last-minute changes by the lawyers. In one recent situation, changes included items such as "that all warranties and representations will terminate in three months instead of 12 months; that there is to be a line-by-line review of the asset allocation; a change in the annual rent; a change in the option to buy the real estate; and exclusion of certain assets from the sale—all without affecting the sales price." It is enough to kill the deal.

In the words of a friend, "Just because you're negotiating doesn't mean you'll close." For example, I lost the biggest sale I was ever involved in because at the final drafting of the agreement, the seller changed his mind and would not indemnify the buyer for certain conditions that he had previously agreed to.

Having read about all the various ways that deals can fall apart, you may feel that the gods of luck are smiling on you if your deal goes through without too many snags and is not killed. From your end, make sure that whatever paperwork is required will be ready when promised, no matter how much you have to pester your advisers. To your advisers, make sure you say loud and clear: "I want to make sure that there is no foul up, or anything to kill the deal from our end, so I'm asking everyone involved to be careful about what they say and how they say it, and to keep every promise." (Often, someone may say the wrong thing, and that could be enough to kill the deal.)

Somehow, when skeletons are left in the closet, they have a way of coming back to haunt you. It is a mistake to feel that you can procrastinate and leave all the rough problems for the end. If they have to be faced, face them; bring them out in the open so they can be dealt with. They will not go away. Tough problems have to be dealt with using tact, finesse, and a good sense of timing. Remember, negotiation involves persuasion and compromise.

There is nothing wrong with telling your buyer what kind of person you are, what your expectations are, and that you are a nut about punctuality, compromises, and thorough preparation. You stand a good chance of getting what you expect if you tell the other person what it is.

Remember, be alert. And there is always prayer.

Why Companies Do Not Sell

Aside from deals collapsing for the various reasons just discussed, there are more reasons companies do not sell. In fact, many do not even get to the deal-negotiating stage. Intermediaries will tell you that when companies do not sell, it is usually because the price is not reasonable, not competitive in the marketplace. Many owners overvalue their company and price it above the market. This is especially true of first-time sellers, who have unrealistic expectations for the selling price of the company.

Most businesspeople do not know how much their business is worth, or how much to ask for their business. They are lucky if they can find someone to help them make the proper valuation, namely, how the marketplace would perceive the selling price if they wanted to sell their company as a going concern.

Here are some of the reasons why prices are sometimes too high.

An owner may be basing the price on the P/E ratios of the public market. Currently the all-industry P/E average is 16, that is, the stocks are selling for 16 times earnings. Remember:

> *The P/E of a public company is based on the after-tax earnings, not the pretax earnings.*

Or an owner may be using the IRS-mandated valuation methods, which are required in valuing estates and gifts, not in pricing companies.

Or an owner may be getting faulty advice, especially if the accountants or lawyers are not in the stream of deal-making and not familiar with the marketplace.

Or an owner calculates how much he will need for his living expenses and then figures how much he will need to get for his company after tax to give him that level of income.

Or an owner can't forget her first costs that she spent for developing the products for the company, but the company does not have enough current sales and earnings to justify such a price.

When prices are too high, it usually means that the *the company cannot meet the acid test:* There is not enough cash flow for the buyer to expect to pay a salary for himself or for a manager, service the debt, and provide a satisfactory return.

Price is not the only reason companies don't get to the negotiating table. Here are three possible problems that may prevent a sale:

1. Insufficient information is made available to prospective buyers.
2. The wrong prospects are looking at the company, such as people who lack an understanding of the business or who have no ability to close.
3. Subversion by employees: In a recent situation, the manager was bidding low on some accounts in order to lose money—hoping that the widow of the former owner would sell out to him, cheap.

And now, as I conclude this edition of my book, I'd like to leave you on a happy note, and suggest that you review Exhibit 1-1. That should raise your spirits as you continue on your journey toward wealth.

Appendix

Some Frequently Asked Questions About Resources

Q. WHO can help me get some confidential background checks on the principals who want to buy my company, or on someone who wants to sell me a company?

A. Some of the better known investigative consultants are:

Bishop's Services, Inc.
304 Park Avenue South, Suite 302
New York, NY 10010

Fidelifacts
50 Broadway, Suite 1107
New York, NY 10004

Kroll Associates
900 Third Avenue
New York, NY 10022

Dun & Bradstreet for Credit History Reporting

Q. If I would like to locate a broker, finder, or merger intermediary, how do I find one?

A. Try your banker, accountant, a friend who has bought or sold a company, or your lawyer. If they can't help:

1. Try to find an active SBIC involved in financing deals, to see who they might recommend.
2. For mid-sized companies, try either of the following and see if they can recommend someone or send you a membership list:

International Merger and Acquisition Professionals (IMAP)
60 Revere Drive, Suite 500
North Brook, IL 60062

International Business Brokers Association
11250 Roger Bacon Drive, Suite 8
Reston, VA 22090

Or perhaps you can locate a regional association.

Q. Are there any newsletters you can tell me about?

A. Here are some newsletters for you to investigate:

Business and Acquisition Newsletter
2600 S. Gessner Road
Houston, TX 77063

National Review of Corporate Acquisitions
Acquisition Resource Corp.
49 Main Street
Tiburon, CA 94920

This is a weekly newsletter with information on larger companies, whether privately held or divestitures.

Buyouts
Securities Data Publishing Co.
40 W. 57th Street
New York, NY 10019

Mostly about upper-middle market, management buyouts, leveraged acquisitions and special situations, and other important news.

The Business Broker
Business Brokerage Press
118 Silver Hill Road
Concord, MA 01742

Its target audience seems to be brokers for small businesses, but it is normally a gold mine of information that would be of interest to a buyer or seller of a small business.

Quality Services Co.
5290 Overpass Road
Santa Barbara, CA 93111

The company publishes a weekly newsletter, and annual transactions of mergers and acquisitions in mostly the public market.

Q. Where can I find lists of companies available for acquisition, and companies seeking acquisitions?

A. Two well-known quarterly editions are:

First List
Vision Quest Publishing, Inc.
655 Rockland Road, Suite 103
Lake Bluff, IL 60044

World M & A Network
International Executive Reports
717 D St., N.W., Suite 300
Washington, DC 20004-2007

Q. Are there any online services or databases, if I want to use my computer and communications software to get listings of small or medium-size businesses?

A. Contact:

> Business Opportunities ON-LINE, Inc.
> 65 First Ave., Suite 202
> Atlantic Highlands, NJ 07716

Q. I'm part of a management group that has an opportunity to acquire our company, but we don't have enough money to do the deal. How can I get information about venture capital companies who might buy the company and work out an equity position for us?

A. Contact:

> Van Kirk's Venture Capital Directory
> c/o Assets Alternative Co.
> 180 Linden Street, Suite 3
> Wellesley, MA 02181
> (800) 257-2947

Available in print or on disk.

Q. Are there any other sources of information you recommend?

A. Those at the high end of the market might want to look at reports and magazines to read what the "big players" have to say. Look into:

> *Mergers and Acquisitions* (bimonthly)
> *Mergers and Acquisitions Report* (weekly)
> *Mergers and Acquisitions International*

Inquire at:

> IDD
> 2 World Trade Center, 18th Floor
> New York, NY 10048

An outstanding resource of ratios, price/cash flow, and return to investors about specific industries and 700 public companies on diskette for PC-compatibles:

Contact:

Media General Finance Services
301 East Grace Street
Richmond, VA 23219

An outstanding reference book is Dun & Bradstreet's *Industry Norms and Key Business Ratios on Over 800 Kinds of Businesses*. They provide ratios on solvency, efficiency, and profitability. Very useful for small to midsize companies.

Publishers of *Annual Merger & Acquisition Source Book*
Write for a list of their publications:

Quality Services Company
5290 Overpass Road, #128
Santa Barbara, CA 93111

Glossary

auction sales   A way of knowing the value of something on a given day. In an absolute auction, the sale goes to the highest bidder. In a reserve auction, the seller has the right to reject bids that do not meet minimum levels. A "bake-off" auction held by investment bankers is sometimes called a controlled or silent auction, where the prospective buyers are asked to make binding bids for a company (many times without contingencies about "not subject to financing").

auction value   In an appraisal, this is something to be sold at public auction within 60 days of the appraisal report. Fair market liquidation value is for items to be sold over an extended period from six to 18 months.

A Dutch auction is generally used to sell commodities, and flowers, and sometimes a business. The seller sets a high price and then starts lowering it until a buyer buys. The first one who bids wins. (Do not confuse this with the technique in the public marketplace of acquiring shares with different pricing levels under a tender offer.)

ball-park figure   The figure asked for by some buyers who are inquiring about how much the company might be offered for, or how much it would take to put them into the game.

B.I.G. (financial) statement   A belief in God statement.

buyer's investment   The equity plus the total of the interest-bearing debt.

buying the balance sheet   The seller guarantees the net worth of the selling company, including the net value of the working capital. If at the closing the net working capital is lower than the original presented, the seller makes up the difference, generally with cash.

cash flow

Cash flow—The pretax net income (profits) plus depreciation, depletion, amortization, and deferred taxes (items that reduce income, without using any cash).

Free cash flow—What is left over after deducting capital expenditures needed to maintain the current level of operations from the cash flow.

Operating cash flow—The amount after you add back to the pretax income the interest paid, taxes paid, and depreciation, like EBDIT. It is what is available before debt and capital expenditures.

   Positive cash flow—More comes in than goes out.
   Negative cash flow—More goes out than come in.
   Zero cash flow—What comes in goes out.

cash in   What happens when the investors take a company to an IPO (initial public offering) and their investment explodes exponentially.

cash out   Straightforward sale for cash, equity, or tax-free stock deal with no restrictions.

check writer   A buyer who can write out a check for $5 million.

C.I.A.   Cash in advance.

closing power or cash buyer   One who has the ability and financial capacity to close a deal because he has the necessary cash or credit.

contingency payment   See *earn-out.*

covenant   What the parties to the purchase and sales agreement promise to do, and promise not to do.

crisis manager   One who is brought in to stabilize a company in the short term. He or she is generally succeeded by a "turn-around manager" to make the company profitable.

divestiture   The sale of a business, division, or subsidiary by a corporate owner to another party.

do a deal   Means the same as to make a deal or close a deal.

due diligence   What lawyers and accountants do after the letter of intent in order to reach the purchase and sales agreement. They look under every rock and in every corner to make sure there are no unexpected negatives.

earn-out   A way of compensating the seller based on future earnings. Additional payments are made if earnings exceed agreed-upon levels. Generally, a reasonable price will be paid for the company up-front with a premium to be paid later.

EBIT   Earnings before interest and taxes.

EBDIT   Earnings before depreciation, interest, and taxes.

entrepreneur   The person who owns and runs the business (from the French for "to undertake"). My description of an entrepreneur: a risk taker, with a high level of energy, a work-aholic, opinionated, hard to work for, but with an attitude that "it" can happen.

expert   Someone who has done something once.

fair market value   The classic definition follows: "The price at which the property would change hands between a willing buyer and a willing seller, when the former is not under any compulsion to buy, and the latter is not under any compulsion to sell, both parties having reasonable knowledge of the facts. The assumption is that the transaction is for cash."

fairness letter   When issued by an investment banker, it supports an opinion that the offer to buy is fair. It generally protects the board of directors in their legal obligation to the stockholders.

f/c   Free and clear, owing no interest-bearing debt.

financial buccaneer   A big risk taker, who operates with big leverage and who might even use fraud if things go wrong.

finder   One who brings a buyer and seller together but is not involved in any negotiation.

first number   In the parlance of some buyers, it is the opening offer, their first price.

floor price   A seller's bottom price beyond which he or she will not lower the price.

full price   The maximum price one should pay for a company—a price with little or no room for error. (See also *walk-away price*.)

G.A.A.P.   As seen in financial statements, meaning, generally accepted accounting principles.

G.S. and A.   General, selling, and administrative expenses.

general utilities doctrine   No longer in effect. It was repealed with the Tax Reform Act of 1986. Prior to that, it was allowed under tax law for the owner of a corporation to arrange his affairs so as to have a nontaxable liquidation. That has all been changed. Now if you sell the assets of a corporation at a gain, first the company must pay the tax on the gain, and then the shareholder liquidates stock and pays a tax on the gain. All together, the taxes including any state taxes could be more than 50% of the gain.

goodwill   In accounting, the difference between the purchase price of a company acquired and the book value. Popularly called "blue sky" or "key" money. The popular definition states that goodwill is that quality of a company that encourages a customer to return where he or she was well treated the previous time.

hard book (hard book value)   When the numbers are not expected to change radically in the near future. Expect stable performance in future as before.

hurdle rate   A minimum acceptable rate for the return on investment.

income

Active income—Money earned from personal business efforts.

Portfolio income—Income from interest, dividends, royalties, annuities; that is, from investments at risk.

Passive income—All other income that is not active or portfolio income.

incremental fixed capital investment   For plant and equipment, the amount over and above depreciation charges.

incremental working capital investment   This reflects the increase in accounts receivable, inventory, and accounts payable required to support a growth in sales.

indemnification   A clause that states what it will cost the seller if the seller breaches a representation. Many times, part of the sales price is held in escrow for a period to cover the indemnification payment. It can cover such items as suits, IRS claims, and fraudulent statements.

intermediary   Brings a buyer and seller together, and may be involved in the negotiations. May or may not be involved in planning, searching, valuation, financing, writing business plans, or preparing profiles.

invested capital   Debt plus equity.

junk bond   A high-risk bond with a rating below BBB.

kentucky windage   An off-of-the-top-of-the-head dreamer's price for a company.

letter of intent   Generally, a letter from a prospective buyer to a seller that he or she intends to buy the company under certain conditions. It is an expression of interest and serves as a guide. It ties up the seller (who agrees to take the property off the market for X days). It does not tie up the buyer, since it is not a binding offer or a commitment.

leveraged recapitalization in a small company   The owner sells part of his or her interest to outside investors, and to his or her own manager in an employee stock ownership plan (ESOP). It still permits the owner to run the company.

liberal arts buyer   One not confined to any special industry, as long as the company meets specific criteria, for example, earnings floor $1 million, stable earnings, and management in place.

liquidation value   Cash left after all the assets are sold and the liabilities are paid off. Could be used as a collateral figure when looking for financing.

loans

Asset based—Based on the tangible assets of the company. The bank might lend: 80% on accounts receivable

60% on inventory

50–70% on plant and equipment

Cash-flow loan—Based on the ability to consistently generate cash from the operations. The bank would expect repayment in five to seven years.

Bridge loan—A temporary loan used to make the deal work until the buyer has a chance to sell some assets, or until some subordinated debt financing can be put in place (usually 4–5 points over prime, with a kicker of 10–25%, plus fees).

Revolver loan—Three-to-seven-year loan. Repayment to begin at once under a schedule.

Evergreen loan—Loan made with no repayment schedule; really a demand loan.

Mezzanine debt or mezzanine financing—Unsecured loan, on a short-term basis, subordinated, until permanent financing can be placed.

market price   What buyers with the financial capacity to close are willing to pay.

merchant banker   A firm that uses its own money to finance deals, either debt or equity.

merger   Company X and company Y combine to form company Z.

note   A written promise to pay, describing the terms and the payments.

parallel negotiations   Dealing with several buyers at one time up to the letter of intent, or the purchase and sales agreement.

pari-passu basis   In a joint venture, it means on a dollar-to-dollar basis.

payment by chip   A new way of speeding up the payment. Actually it is payment using a coded disk, issued by the bank against which the funds are drawn. When the papers are all set and signed and the funds are ready to be paid, the disk relays data by modem, and the payment is transferred to the seller's account any hour of the day, bypassing the Federal Reserve.

platform company   When entrepreneurs buy a company ($10–20 million) and use it as a platform to acquire other similarly small companies and bring them to a size that can go to the public market. The investors can bring strategic planning skills, marketing skills, and financial controls to smaller companies.

pretax income   The starting point for calculating the EBIT figure.

success fee   Payable only when a task or transaction is completed.

tender offer   A legal binding offer to purchase stock from shareholders. Sometimes it can carry restrictions and contingencies.

thirty-eight   The magic number for venture capitalists, where they aspire to 38% annual IRR (internal rate of return). At this rate their investment (not including debt) will multiply five times in five years if they sell the company, go public, or recapitalize (borrow) so they can dividend out.

value According to Karl Marx, value is what is socially necessary. It is the labor time to create the product.

value in exchange Value to the prospective buyer.

value in use Value to the owner.

walk-away price A price that, when reached, takes the buyer above his or her previously decided upper limit, and he or she walks away from the deal.

winner's curse When the most optimistic buyer wins, but only because he or she paid too much for the company.

Reading List

Annual Merger & Acquisition Source Book. Santa Barbara, CA: Quality Services Company, annual.

Baron, Paul. *When You Buy or Sell a Company: How to Price and How to Negotiate, Revised Edition.* Stony Creek, CT: Center for Business Administration, 1986.

Bunn, Verne A. *Buying and Selling a Small Business.* Salem, NH: Ayer, 1979.

Bruck, Connie. *The Predator's Ball.* New York: Simon & Schuster, 1988.

Federal Estate and Gift Tax Reports, IRS Appellate Conferee Valuation Training Program. Report number 49. Chicago: Commerce Clearing House.

Industry Norms and Key Business Ratios on Over 800 Kinds of Businesses. New York: Dun & Bradstreet.

Kohler, Eric L. *A Dictionary for Accountants, Fifth Edition.* Englewood Cliffs, NJ: Prentice-Hall, 1975.

Index